Relationship and Resource Management in Operations

Butterworth-Heinemann – The Securities Institute

A publishing partnership

About the Securities Institute

Formed in 1992 with the support of the Bank of England, the London Stock Exchange, the Financial Services Authority, LIFFE and other leading financial organizations, the Securities Institute is the professional body for practitioners working in securities, investment management, corporate finance, derivatives and related businesses. Their purpose is to set and maintain professional standards through membership, qualifications, training and continuing learning and publications. The Institute promotes excellence in matters of integrity, ethics and competence.

About the series

Butterworth-Heinemann is pleased to be the official **Publishing Partner** of the Securities Institute with the development of professional level books for: Brokers/Traders; Actuaries; Consultants; Asset Managers; Regulators; Central Bankers; Treasury Officials; Compliance Officers; Legal Departments; Corporate Treasurers; Operations Managers; Portfolio Managers; Investment Bankers; Hedge Fund Managers; Investment Managers; Analysts and Internal Auditors, in the areas of: Portfolio Management; Advanced Investment Management; Investment Management Models; Financial Analysis; Risk Analysis and Management; Capital Markets; Bonds; Gilts; Swaps; Repos; Futures; Options; Foreign Exchange; Treasury Operations.

Series titles

■ **Professional Reference Series**
   The Bond and Money Markets: *Strategy, Trading, Analysis*

■ **Global Capital Markets Series**
   The REPO Handbook
   Foreign Exchange and Money Markets: *Theory, Practice and Risk Management*
   IPO and Equity Offerings
   European Securities Markets Infrastructure
   Best Execution in the Integrated Securities Market

■ **Operations Management Series**
   Clearing, Settlement and Custody
   Controls, Procedures and Risk
   Relationship and Resource Management in Operations
   Managing Technology in the Operations Function
   Regulation and Compliance in Operations
   Understanding the Markets

For more information

For more information on **The Securities Institute** please visit their web site:

   www.securities-institute.org.uk

and for details of all **Butterworth-Heinemann Finance** titles please visit Butterworth-Heinemann:

   www.bh.com/finance

Relationship and Resource Management in Operations

David Loader

BUTTERWORTH
HEINEMANN

OXFORD AMSTERDAM BOSTON LONDON NEW YORK PARIS
SAN DIEGO SAN FRANCISCO SINGAPORE SYDNEY TOKYO

332.10681
L79r

Butterworth-Heinemann
An imprint of Elsevier Science
Linacre House, Jordan Hill, Oxford OX2 8DP
200 Wheeler Road, Burlington MA 01803

First published 2002

British Library Cataloguing in Publication Data
A catalogue record for this book is available from the British Library

Library of Congress Cataloguing in Publication Data
A catalogue record for this book is available from the Library of Congress

ISBN 0 7506 5488 0

For information on all Butterworth-Heinemann finance publications
visit our website at: www.bh.com/finance

Composition by Genesis Typesetting, Rochester, Kent
Printed and bound in Great Britain

Contents

Preface

The Operations function in a financial organization is crucial to the success of the business. It drives both profitability and reputation as well as contributing to business development and support. It is also a complex part of a business and one that is treated differently in different types of organization. Often considered a service or support function, it can equally be designated as a profit centre or revenue generator. The Operations function itself is made up of many processes that are either standalone or part of a multi-process function, but all the processes are linked to other processes elsewhere in the organization and/or outside of it.

The complexity of Operations and the diverseness of the teams and the people they interact with creates a need for a high degree of relationship and resource management. A bank, for instance, that has both retail and investment banking will have hundreds of different relationship situations but so too will a small private client broker. Some situations may be common to all types of organization, others similar for certain types of organization and a few will be very specific to an organization. These relationships may be very open or highly discreet and confidential.

Whatever the type of relationship it is fairly obvious that any problems are likely to have an impact on the business and so too will successful relationships.

Take, for instance, the client of a bank. What matters to them? What is the basis for a successful relationship? Retail banks in the UK ran into a high degree of client resentment at the closure of local branches. The policy may have made financial sense to the banks but it angered the clients and certainly in one case, NatWest, the policy was reversed.

Likewise if a large organization runs into a period of lower profits and returns to shareholders it often takes steps to 'rationalize' its cost base. This, in virtually every case, means reducing head-count and/or reducing expenditure on systems and/or development. The action may achieve the desired result of reducing the cost base but at what cost to the business? If the reductions result in delays in delivery and the quality and response time to customers then almost certainly the impact will be to increase losses as frustrated customers take their business elsewhere. Too often the importance of adequate resource levels and the recognition of how vital relationship management can be is lost in the 'facts and figures' produced by the accountants and consultants.

Another example of the problem with relationship management, and in particular the client or customer relationship, is the use of help desks and call centres. The logic is fine; receive the inquiry in a central place and route it to the person that can deal with it. The reality is that many people do not want to listen to recordings telling them to press buttons and so there is an immediate resentment where perhaps the caller had none before.

It is tempting to assume that relationship management is about clients and resource management about head-count. That is not the case.

In the early days of the Industrial Revolution when engineering and production processes became the heart of industry, the key to success was the linking together of processes to form a continuous process. The production or assembly line concept was created and worked only if each part of the line completed its task efficiently so that the next part of the line could start its task. This required a high degree of coordination and conformity. Each person doing a task had to be able to do it as well as each other, i.e. uniform skill levels, and there had to be enough people to ensure the task was always being done, i.e. adequate human resource level. There also had to be a continuous supply of the raw material and a means to store and distribute the end product, i.e. resource supply and infrastructure, as well as a market for the goods, i.e. sales, marketing and client relationship.

It is easy to see the potential problems.

- Problems with production but highly successful sales
- High production but poor sales
- Good productivity and sales but poor supply of raw material
- Good production and sales but poor distribution
- High demand but difficulty in getting resource
- Poor-quality products leading to loss of sales
- Ability to increase production and sales but not storage and distribution

So not only is the relationship issue with the customer and the number of people in the workforce important, so too is the relationship with the supplier of the raw material, the different sections on the production line, the storage capacity and distribution, sales and marketing. There is so much interdependency that resource and relationship management is just simply crucial to the success of the business.

When we apply this to the financial markets we are essentially talking about a production line that moves from trading through clearing and settlement and into added-value services. Each is dependent on the other and the quality is vital if the customer is to be gained and/or retained. Equally important is the impact on the profitability of the business.

We have then several resource and relationship issues to consider. Broadly speaking, these could include:

External relationships
- Markets/exchanges
- Clearing houses

- Depositories
- Clients (members for exchanges and clearing-houses)
- Custodians
- Trustees
- Independent financial advisors
- Regulators
- Audit
- Prime brokers
- Fund administration
- Banks and payment systems
- System suppliers
- Service companies
- Information suppliers

Internal relationships
- Dealers/traders
- Fund managers
- Middle office/operations
- Client relationship teams
- Corporate finance
- Treasury
- Fund administration
- Retail sales and distribution
- Branch/subsidiary offices
- Audit
- Compliance
- Risk management group
- Technology
- Board/senior management
- Premises and services
- Human resources

There are, I have no doubt, many more that the reader could identify for their particular organization, but the general point is that relationships within and without organizations are a fairly complex business where they may be direct or indirect and several relationships may apply for a particular circumstance.

For example if we look at a unit trust we have at least the following potential relationships:

- Fund manager to dealer
- Dealer to operations
- Operations and fund administration
- Fund admin/Ops to custodian
- Fund admin/custodian to trustee
- Fund manager to trustee
- Fund admin/Ops/custodian to payment systems and banks
- Fund manager to marketing and sales
- Marketing and independent financial advisors
- Sales and distribution to the customer
- Help desk to customer

In this example each of the above has specific roles in the process. It needs to work well for the unit trust to be successfully sold to the customers and, of course, to ensure that the trust complies with the regulation over the business, the scheme particulars, etc. It is also vital so that the assets of the unit trust are bought and sold, successfully settled and recorded as well as being valued correctly for input to the pricing of the units.

In more simplistic terms the good relationship between front office (dealers/traders/fund managers) and Operations is crucial for the control of risk and maximizing of profitability (reducing of loss) of each trade. So too is the relationship between Operations and custodians and depositories so that any problems with settlement flows, cash or asset movements, etc. can be quickly resolved with minimal disruption and cost.

Vitally important is the relationship between the operating units and their colleagues in technology. Technology drives every part of the financial services industry so relationship failures or resource problems in this area will just simply have a detrimental impact on the business.

Having stressed how important it all is, what happens if it does go wrong? I suppose the answer here is really about to what extent there is a breakdown in relationships or for how long there is a resource problem. The longer it runs and more embedded the problem becomes, the more vulnerable the organization is. At some point the problems will manifest themselves into a more significant risk issue and ultimately could mean the demise of a company.

For the Operations managers their role is a key one. Charged with managing resource and the numerous relationship issues, it is neither a simple task nor, because of variety and frequency of the issues that might arise, is it one that is easy to find solutions.

We will explore some of the situations that managers might find themselves in as we move through the book. The most important thing to stress is that every business and every manager is different. There is, in theory, no definitive method of managing relationships, some being specific ones and some being ones that can and will change as personnel come and go or business profiles change.

Personalities obviously play a major part in the relationship process being both productive and counterproductive. Skills are also vital, both personal and technical. As far as managers and supervisors are concerned, communicative skills are crucial as many a problem has occurred because of a misunderstanding!

This also applies to resource management as the case for a new infrastructure or expenditure of a resource may be proven but the ability to present the argument to senior management or the budget committee and win funding is not so straightforward.

Relationships and resource are the energy source that makes Operations work. Managed well they will provide the means to grow and to attain success.

Chapter 1

Understanding the business – the role of Operations

Operations sections, teams or departments today have a very varied role in an organization. Standard tasks and functions associated with the clearing, settlement, administration and support of trading, banking and investment activity form the core activities of these teams. However, within banks and brokers in many cases this traditional role has been expanded to encompass elements of revenue generation, third-party administration services and a wide range of client-related services.

Of course, some organizations have the provision of these type of services as their core business. Custodians, clearing houses, fund administrators and central securities depositories, for instance, are organizations that develop and deliver services and generate their income from this activity rather than trading and investment.

Because there is great diversity in the role of the Operations function, in a particular organization this role must be understood if the resource and relationships that it has are to be managed successfully.

Operations teams are both part of a larger structure and will also have structures of their own. In simple generic terms the structure in a bank or broker could be as shown in Figures 1.1 or 1.2.

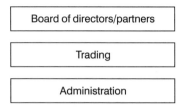

Figure 1.1 Structure of a bank or broker: 1

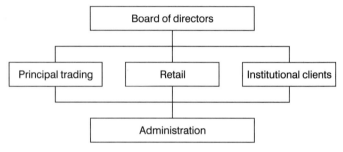

Figure 1.2 Structure of a bank or broker: 2

However, a bank is likely to be structured along business and/or product lines so that the structure may look more like Figure 1.3.

If the organization was a fund management company the structure might appear as in Figure 1.4.

It is fairly obvious that the Operations function fits the business profile of the organization and it should therefore be equally obvious that Operations is a business in its own right.

The business of Operations

What is the business profile of Operations?

The core business is the processing, recording and settlement of instructions related to transactions. This is provided across a range of products and markets, often domestic and internationally, and

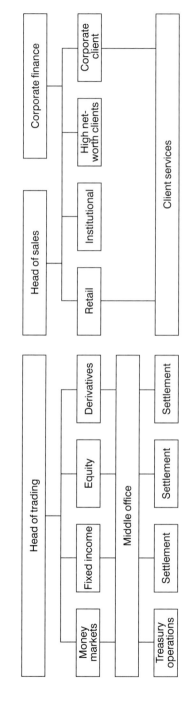

Figure 1.3 Structure of a bank along business and/or product lines

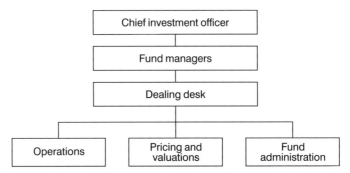

Figure 1.4 Structure of a fund management company

involves standard processes and procedures as determined by the market conventions and regulations.

The Operations function must comply with both internal and external accounting requirements, regulation, controls, and reporting and risk management requirements. This will include maintaining accurate records related to the transactions being processed.

The non-core business is the provision of sundry services that offer clients standard or bespoke solutions related to their specific business requirements. It is important to recognize that an Operations function in an organization can have both internal and external clients and the services provided to each may well be very different. The internal clients will be the trading desks, corporate finance, etc. or in the case of a fund management company the individual managers and the dealing desks.

Core business

For the core business it is imperative that suitable resource must be provided, resource that is both adequate and competent to meet the procedures necessary for dealing with the processes. The cost of providing this resource is crucial, as it becomes a part of the overall business cost and, more specifically, the cost of transaction or bargain. Equally there will be regulatory requirements covering competency standards, systems and experience as well as procedures and controls that must be in place for this core business. Any failures in this respect may result in a licence to do business being revoked or not granted.

The core business areas would include:

- Data capture
- Instructions
- Settlement
- Record keeping
- Maintenance of records and reconciliation
- Funding and asset management
- Accounting
- Valuation
- Client and regulatory reporting

To provide the core business there will be a normal business structure of management, supervisors and personnel. The human resource may be specialist or generalist and the Operations structure itself have both vertical and horizontal links (see Figure 1.5).

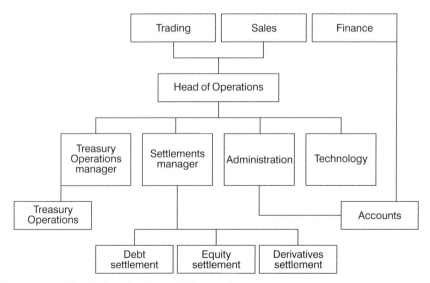

Figure 1.5 Vertical or horizontal Operations structure

Non-core business

Most of the non-core business areas relate to the additional or non-standard services that are provided. These can include a very diverse range of products from technology-based system services to information provision and even training. The non-core business is often branded and can even be provided by a separate area such as 'client services'. In some cases the core and non-core Operations business is incorporated into specific vehicles so that we have fund administration companies, prime brokers and derivative clearers.

Non-core business in terms of custody, for instance, would be termed added-value services and might include:

- Withholding tax
- Performance management
- Reporting
- Cash management
- Market information

Service supplier or revenue centre?

Traditionally the Operations function has been an administration or service part of the overall business rather than being seen as a revenue generator or profit centre. The cost of Operations, often referred to as a cost centre, was charged to the profit centres and often this was on a general rather than product- or market-specific basis. The end result was that the cost of the Operations function was viewed as a 'necessary evil' rather than any focus on the business benefits of Operations or accurate profit/loss data on markets and products. The costs of administration being not directly related to the revenue centres was a situation that inevitably led to arguments between the different parts of the business as to whether the costs were reasonable and to a generally negative view of the administration function.

Today the Operations function is very likely to be a profit centre in its own right and as a business it needs to be aware of the same financial and competitive pressures and issues under which the front office operates. The cost of Operations is reflected in a fee or charge per bargain that can be easily compared to the charge made by an external organization. Equally benchmarks enable the service offered by the Operations teams to be measured and, of course, there are no shortage of organizations offering outsourcing services that enable an organization to dispense with all or most of its Operations functions. There are many arguments for and against outsourcing and these are looked at later in the book.

As a consequence of this the Operations business is very much about quality and costs in a competitive environment.

Business issues

As there is a clear emphasis on quality and cost one key issue facing Operations is the ability to budget accurately for the overheads and cost of resources needed to provide the services offered while at the same time reflecting a competitive price for the services.

A great opportunity and indeed temptation would be to subsidize the cost of Operations to internal clients by charging a higher fee to external clients. There are two problems with this. First, the internal clients will not want fluctuating costs, so what happens if revenue from external clients falls? Second, the external client charges will need to be competitive with the market. Over the years the level of fee that can be charged has fallen as competition has increased and client resistance to high fees has materialized. This can be illustrated by looking at how the number of organizations offering custody services has decreased as pressure on fee levels combined with soaring costs of maintaining systems and resource to deliver the service increases. In many cases there was no longer a justification for being in what was rapidly becoming a very marginal business. Those custody providers that remain benefit from the reduction in players as fee levels stabilize with less competition and the remaining businesses pick up critical mass, and higher fees, as clients move from those withdrawing from the market.

Organizations like banks that offer outsource facilities are utilizing their existing internal infrastructure and in effect are bringing down the net cost of Operations to the in-house businesses. The cost of upgrading the systems to cover the changes and development in the business and the industry can be prohibitive if the system's use is not maximized.

Operations managers have to understand finance and the cost of money. They need to be able to budget for resource, running costs, volumes, future development, staff training and development, etc.

The business issues are such an important part of the role of managers and, without adequate training and skills, dealing with such issues will be difficult. The solution is for firms to have active and structured development programmes for managers and indeed many do. Just as important, however, is ensuring that Operations staff also have adequate training in business skills as well as the technical skills they need. Without this we have a risk that weaknesses will occur in the overall Operations function, its processes, procedures and controls.

Operational risk

Another significant business issue for Operations is operational risk. However, we need to be careful to differentiate between operational risk and operations risk. There are many definitions of both and we look at an example shortly. It is important to the development and delivery of Operations-based services that operational and operations risks are considered. Relationships, skill sets, resource levels, procedures and controls are all areas that can be a cause of risk and/or affected by risk. This in turn leads to an impact on the business of Operations.

Operational risk is about identifying and minimizing the risk of errors and losses and preventing situations where the reputation of the business is affected. It is also about the need to manage the Operations and operational functions in such a way that the overall risk capital requirement is kept as low as possible.

By effectively managing risk in Operations the manager is having a positive impact on the risk management of the whole business and at the same time is creating the environment where an efficient and cost-effective function will operate.

Working paper on the regulatory treatment of operational risk

Abstract

The purpose of this paper prepared by the Risk Management Group of the Basel Committee is to further the Committee's dialogue with the industry on the development of a Pillar 1 capital charge for operational risk in the New Basel Capital Accord. Comments on the issues outlined in this paper would be welcome, and should be submitted to relevant national supervisory authorities and central banks and may also be sent to the Secretariat of the Basel Committee on Banking Supervision at the Bank for International Settlements, CH-4002 Basel, Switzerland, by 31 October 2001. Comments may be submitted via e-mail: BCBS.capital@bis.org or by fax: +41 61 280 9100. Comments on working papers will not be posted on the BIS website.

Introduction, definitions and data issues

Background and the rationale for an operational risk charge

In recent years, supervisors and the banking industry have recognized the importance of operational risk in shaping the risk profiles of financial institutions. Developments such as the use of more highly automated technology, the growth of e-commerce, large-scale mergers and acquisitions that test the viability of newly integrated systems, the emergence of banks as very large-volume service providers, the increased prevalence of outsourcing and the greater use of financing techniques that reduce credit and market risk, but that create increased operational risk, all suggest that operational risk exposures may be substantial and growing.

This recognition has led to an increased emphasis on the importance of sound operational risk management at financial institutions and to greater prominence of operational risk in banks' internal capital assessment and allocation processes. In fact, the banking industry is currently undergoing a surge of innovation and development in these areas.

Reflecting these developments, the Basel Committee on Banking Supervision established the principle of developing a Pillar 1 minimum regulatory capital charge for other risk, including operational risk, in its 1999 Consultative Paper. Following the consultation process and its own analysis, the Committee decided that only operational risk should be subject to a capital charge under Pillar 1. Additional elements of 'other risk' – for instance, interest rate risk in the banking book and liquidity risk – will be dealt with solely through Pillars 2 and 3. This position was expressed in the January 2001 Consultative Package and forms the assumption underpinning the Risk Management Group's (RMG's) ongoing analysis.

This paper contains an overview of the RMG's work to date on refining the proposals for a Pillar 1 regulatory minimum capital requirement for operational risk. It reflects the RMG's extensive contact with financial industry representatives, its review of the many thoughtful and constructive comments received on the January Consultative Package, and the RMG's own internal deliberations. This work has resulted in a number of significant changes to the January proposals. These changes include:

- Refinement of the definition of operational risk that underpins the regulatory capital calculations;
- Proposed reduction in the overall level of the operational risk capital charge;
- Introduction of a new regulatory capital approach that is based on banks' internal risk estimates (the 'Advanced Measurement Approaches' [AMA]); and

■ Consideration of the role of insurance as a risk mitigant in the regulatory capital calculations.

These changes are described more fully in the sections that follow. The RMG intends to continue work to refine these proposals in light of industry comments and with the benefit of tranche 2 Quantitative Impact Study (QIS) data that it will review further over the course of the autumn.

Definition of operational risk

In the January 2001 Consultative Package, operational risk was defined as: 'the risk of direct or indirect loss resulting from inadequate or failed internal processes, people and systems or from external events'. The January 2001 paper went on to clarify that this definition included legal risk, but that strategic and reputational risks were not included in this definition for the purpose of a minimum regulatory operational risk capital charge.

This focus on operational risk has been generally welcomed, although concerns were expressed about the exact meaning of 'direct and indirect loss'. As mentioned above, for the purposes of a Pillar 1 capital charge, strategic and reputational risks are not included, and neither is it the intention for the capital charge to cover all indirect losses or opportunity costs. As a result, reference to 'direct and indirect' in the overall definition has been dropped. By directly defining the types of loss events that should be recorded in internal loss data, the RMG can give much clearer guidance on which losses are relevant for regulatory capital purposes. This leads to a slightly revised definition, as follows: **'the risk of loss resulting from inadequate or failed internal processes, people and systems or from external events'**. The RMG confirms that this definition does not include systemic risk and the operational risk charge will be calibrated accordingly.

It is important to note that this definition is based on the underlying causes of operational risk. It seeks to identify why a loss happened and at the broadest level includes the breakdown by four causes: people, processes, systems and external factors. This 'causal-based' definition, and more detailed specifications of it, is particularly useful for the discipline of managing operational risk within institutions. However, for the purpose of operational risk loss quantification and the pooling of loss data across banks, it is necessary to rely on definitions that are readily measurable and comparable. Given the current state of industry practice, this has led banks and supervisors to move towards the distinction between operational risk causes, actual measurable events (which may be due to a number of causes, many of which may not be fully understood), and the P&L effects (costs) of those events. Operational risk can be analysed at each of these levels.

Data collection

A key issue in the area of operational risk management – as well as in the development of regulatory capital requirements – is the collection and analysis of loss data. Whilst a growing number of institutions are collecting and analysing operational loss data, with some operating internal capital assessment and allocation mechanisms on this basis, it is clear that there has been no industry standard for such data exercises. Such data collection is important for the assessment of operational risk at individual institutions. There is also increasing recognition amongst banks and supervisors that the sharing of loss data, based on consistent definitions and metrics, is necessary to arrive at a comprehensive assessment of operational risk.

The Committee has been keen to incentivize banks to develop further data collection and analysis. The proposal for a Pillar I capital charge has been an important stimulant in this regard, but, more directly, the RMG, via the QIS project, has set in train a data collection exercise that will help calibrate and test the proposed framework for operational risk. This framework, which was established in close collaboration with the banking industry and others, breaks operational risk exposures and losses into a series of standardized business lines and 'event types'. The business lines are intended to be generally applicable across a wide range of institutions.

The event types are intended to group operational risk losses into distinct components according to the nature of the underlying operational risk event. Annex 2 contains the full framework of business lines and event types.

The definitions of event types are intended to encompass certain operational risk losses that currently may be embedded in credit or market risk related exposures. Going forward, the RMG wants to encourage banks to track explicitly these types of operational risk losses to arrive at a comprehensive assessment of the true operational risk profile within and across institutions. The Committee expects banks to include all operational risks in the loss event database and have clear policies implemented for the management of these risks. Nevertheless, for regulatory capital purposes the Committee expects banks to attribute operational risk related credit and market loss events to those risk areas for the calculation of regulatory capital requirements. The Committee will calibrate the overall capital charge for operational risk to prevent double counting with the credit capital charge. Banks should not retroactively seek to strip out operational losses from their existing credit loss databases and calculations in determining their regulatory capital require-ments for credit risk.

There were two strands to the work in the QIS: the first strand provided information on exposure indicators and the economic capital allocation to operational risk by business line. These data were instrumental in allowing the provisional estimate of the relative risk of the business lines and hence a preliminary reporting of the survey results as they relate to the Basic Indicator and Standardised Ap-proaches, using a 'top down' methodology (i.e. a technique where a predetermined amount of capital is allocated across business lines). The results of this analysis are set out below.

The second strand of the QIS aimed to collect loss data from individual banks on a consistent and coherent basis and so allow a 'bottom-up' assessment of all three approaches to operational risk capital. This tranche of the survey will also allow exploration of the issue of 'double counting' operational risk, as discussed above. Additional analysis of this tranche of QIS will continue over the autumn and will be reflected in further output from the Committee.

Source: Basel Committee

So managers clearly need to manage aspects of the resource and relationships with Operations and operational risk in mind.

The policy of the firm will to some extent dictate this. One area of risk management is managing changes and there is, in most markets in the world, significant change taking place in how markets operate and in the infrastructures that support the business such as clearing and custody.

As the system, procedures, processes and controls are amended and updated the management of resource and relationships will come under intense pressure. Logistics delays/difficulties with implementation of change will all be problems that have to be overcome.

In these circumstances risk will increase and therefore there is an argument for additional funding for consultants, temporary staff, etc. while the projects are implemented so that the risk element is reduced.

Market and clearing rationalization

Market conventions and regulation determine the clearing and settlement processes. There has been and still is significant change taking place in the industry today and this is affecting these clearing and settlement processes. This then filters through into the business of Operations as procedures and added-value services are adapted and developed to reflect the changes.

There are several significant changes that are affecting the structure of Operations. The central clearing counterparty and netting are two examples. The central clearing counterparty (CCP) concept is not new and has been part of the clearing process of exchange-traded derivatives since the 1800s. The gradual introduction of the CCP to securities clearing has brought the concepts of margin and netting to the forefront of thinking and into the procedures and processes. For some markets like the London Stock Exchange and Eurex the netting issues that concern members has resulted in a dual system of either gross or net settlement. Euronext, on the other hand, will have introduced netting across all its products and markets during 2002. Netting, of course, affects the clearing members more than the non-clearing members of the exchange so the respective Operations teams in these organizations will have different procedures and processes in the workflow. The concept of margin as a deposit against obligations introduces issues surrounding collateral. The relationships in the CCP environment can be as illustrated in Figure 1.6.

These changes to the structure of clearing and settlement coupled with those in the regulatory and risk management process are presenting both challenges and risks. Resource skills are changing to reflect the automation and globalization of the Operations business. As the process of doing business speeds up through electronic markets and straightthrough processing initiatives, the need for data-processing personnel is replaced with a need for exception managers, risk monitors and client services people.

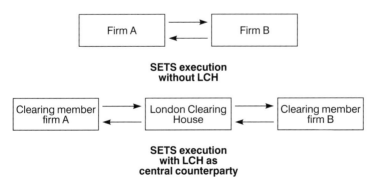

Figure 1.6 Relationships in the CCP environment. (*Source*: The London Clearing House)

The latter is vitally important. In-house and external clients must be provided with the highest quality of source and as the changes we have talked about in this chapter happen so the Operations team must adopt to the changing demands of the client base.

The role of Operations in tomorrow's world

Change, change and more change sums up the world of Operations now and for the foreseeable future. It is vital that managers and supervisors have vision and the ability to plan ahead and set in motion changes that will be needed such as retraining. Given the unprecedented growth and globalization of the business together with the plethora of new products and users, it is even more crucial that Operations managers and teams are business orientated and addressing the issues of tomorrow today. That is not always easy and, as we see in a later chapter, implementing change can be extremely difficult if people are fearful or opposed to the change. Nevertheless, it is part of the manager's role and therefore one on which they will be judged. The business of Operations is just that, a business.

Chapter 2

Operations relationships in the organization

Introduction

Any organization, however large or small, only thrives if there is a sense of purpose, pride and contentment prevailing across it. This idyllic situation is unlikely to be there on a constant or permanent basis and will fluctuate as pressures and changes routinely occur. Nevertheless a carefully structured organization that recognizes the collective as well as individual input and issues is more likely to be successful, and more likely to overcome short-term problems than a disjointed group or business units however talented they may be.

In the financial markets there is an environment that presents a very real challenge to the managers. There is a mystique about money and the financial markets in general often enhanced by both the positive thought of being at the very heart of the financial process that drives the domestic and global economy and the negative publicity of events such as the Mirror Group pension scandal and rogue traders and spectacular collapses of firms such as Enron. Then there are also the highly publicized mega-salaries that can be earned. There is also a variable level of business influenced by the economic outlook of countries and continents that leads to often very long hours being worked by many in what is a complex and diverse industry. Money, and how it works, is intriguing to everyone so this volatile cocktail makes the financial markets an exciting and potentially hugely rewarding occupation and attracts recruits from a wide-ranging background. In reality there is a lot of routine, some very tired people and not always the golden egg everyone assumes there will be. This environment described above also includes a whole plethora of mini-challenges that make relationship management one of the most important roles of the Operations manager.

Structures and relationships

As we have already said, there are no set structures for organizations although different types of businesses will have generic structures. A retail bank has a structure quite different from that of a merchant bank and where financial markets are de-regulated and we have investment banks there will be several different structures within the same organization. Although structures may differ, the functions at a high level do not and so we can have the type of generic structure we looked at in Chapter 1.

Simplistically we have a dealing, investment or trading function or functions and a support function. Within the dealing, investment and trading function, or 'front office' as it is usually termed, we have principal and client activity. The client activity may be further broken down into institutional clients, private clients, corporate clients and retail (see Figures 2.1 and 2.2).

Case study

We can look at a hypothetical structure in a global investment bank, Global Bank Inc., to illustrate the complex nature of the business and how the structure within the bank creates a series of support or Operations functions. Structures are usually vertical or horizontal and are related to considerations such as product, client, market,

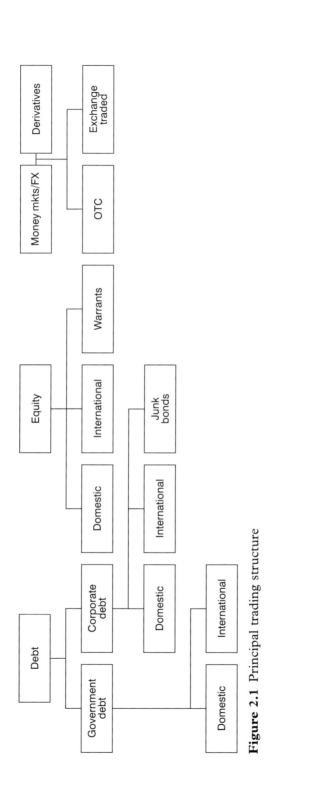

Figure 2.1 Principal trading structure

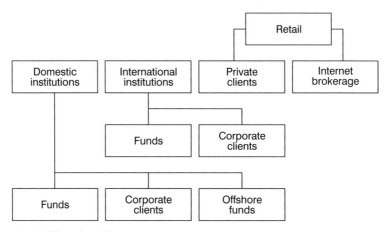

Figure 2.2 Client/retail structure

geographical location, etc. A head office or similarly termed function will exist and, depending on the diversity of the company's business and its global reach, there will be one or more branch, subsidiary or part-owned businesses in other locations. If you get hold of a copy of a major bank's Annual Report you will see just how many branch and/ or subsidiaries and part-owned businesses make up the 'Group'. Many of these companies are established for legal or tax reasons. Some are directly controlled from the head office, others are semi-autonomous and occasionally fully autonomous. The amount of interaction between these various companies may be significant or non-existent. The core business functions do interact: for instance, the fund management business will often utilize various services and products supplied by the principal trading arm of the group such as research or administration.

Within Global Bank Inc. there are several key business areas:

- Trading
- Sales – Retail
- Sales – Institutional
- Corporate Finance
- Operations and Administration

- Treasury and Group Finance
- Compliance
- Accounting and Audit
- Technology

Within each of these there are numerous sub-areas (Figure 2.3).

Global Inc. has a complex and diverse structure in its main office that is replicated either fully or to some degree in its subsidiaries and branches. Even without going into great detail we can deduce that the Operations function and the operational infrastructure to support such a business is going to be complex and diverse. There will be many relationships between the different parts of Global Bank, even where there are departments such as corporate finance that for confidentiality and other reasons are often working in highly secure areas with minimal direct contact with other parts of the bank.

In some organizations that are structured along divisional lines we find that Operations is part of a specific 'operations' or 'settlement' division which may be either a service or cost centre or a revenue centre. We have assumed in the previous figures that Global Bank Inc. has a settlement division. That in turn has a structure and most of the internal relationships will spring from how it is structured.

Structure in Operations

It is perhaps inevitable that within the very large organizations there is an element of duplication of functions, processes and roles within the Operations area. This is particularly the case where we have the vertical product line structures. As the clearing and settlement process in the industry changes, multi-functional Operations teams will replace the vertical product-orientated structure. The rationalization created by straightthrough-processing (STP) is also removing the direct product/support structure.

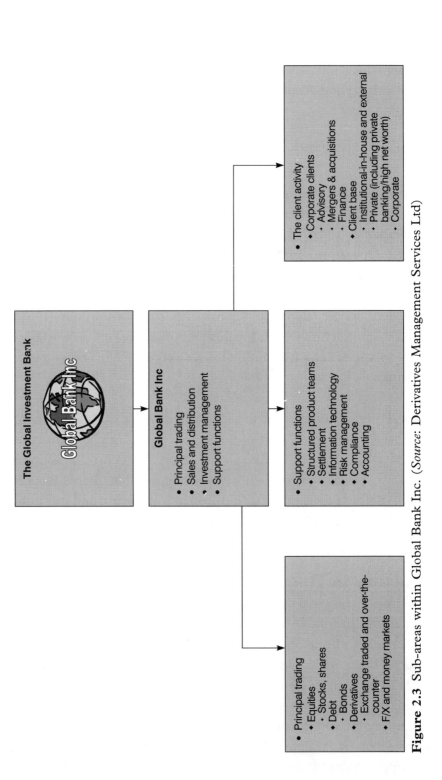

Figure 2.3 Sub-areas within Global Bank Inc. (*Source:* Derivatives Management Services Ltd)

The use of a so-called 'middle office' occurred as firms realized the importance of ensuring adequate support to the dealers and traders but also the need to adequately segregate critical tasks such as profit/loss calculation and asset valuations. Once again there is no particular conformity and 'middle office' in one organization may mean something quite different in another. Many organizations have some element of a 'middle office' function to deal with over-the-counter derivatives, structured products or special-purpose vehicles. Middle office tasks tend to be focused on reconciling dealers' positions, profit and loss and the structure and pricing of products.

In generic terms the Operations relationships could be illustrated by Figures 2.4 and 2.5 that represent the securities and derivatives relationship flow.

Inter-departmental relationships

In Figures 2.4 and 2.5 we see at high level the main links between the functions and departments within those functions. The relationships between these areas will be on a basis of:

- Constant
- Frequent
- Periodic
- Specific

Constant relationships exist between the directly related functions such as trading and trade capture, settlement and treasury, etc. These relationships need high levels of management to ensure that there is efficient and secure processing, that procedures are followed and that issues and problems are raised and solutions found. This is vital as the relationships are interdependent on each other and any deterioration in a core relationship environment will be potentially disastrous for the organization, not least because it creates an operational risk situation.

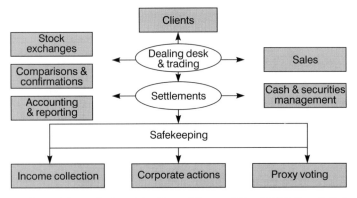

Figure 2.4 Securities relationship flow. (*Source*: The DSC Portfolio)

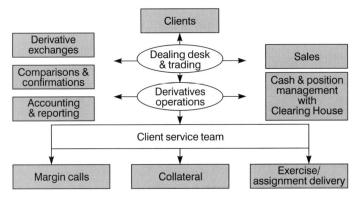

Figure 2.5 Derivatives relationship flow. (*Source*: The DSC Portfolio)

Frequent relationships exist between areas such as corporate actions and the front office/clients while periodic relationships exist between Operations and, say, Audit. Specific relationships occur between, say, corporate finance and different parts of the business or with the client for a single purpose such as a structured product, special vehicle or take-over/merger situation.

The need for the relationship to work is always vital as errors, delays and failure to understand the importance of something will be costly. The more problems, the worse the relationship and the greater the problems; a vicious circle begins and it is desperately difficult to bring things back in line once reputation is damaged and doubts exist.

Within all organizations the critical feature in the success or otherwise of the business is not management skills, technical abilities, capacity, technology or even capital; it is actually communication.

Quite simply, 99% of relationship issues that impact negatively on an organization are entirely or significantly due to communication issues. This is hardly surprising since Operations has as part of its role the receipt of data, the verification and repackaging of data and the distribution of data. As much of that data is sourced from and/or supplied to clients, be they internal or external, any problems will potentially be serious. However, as we have already seen, given the complex structures within organizations and the various departments or sections that complete the process chains the movement of data internally across the business is a crucial process in its own right. The data must be accurate and timely because it is re-used in processes and decisions, hence this interdependency on the component parts of the process. The skills of the teams, supervisors and managers in ensuring that this data is communicated efficiently are the key.

If we take it into a global scenario we have the same situation but with new influences such as time-zones, languages, conventions and culture. Here relationships and their management will have different characteristics and require different approaches, procedures and handling. Responsibility may be shared or at arm's length. Incorporating the standards used in, say, New York or London may be a major problem in a smaller, less-well resourced office elsewhere and yet if the assumption is that the standards are uniform across the organization serious problems can and will occur.

Chapter 3

Operations relationships outside the organization

In the previous chapter we looked at issues surrounding relationships and resource in terms of the internal structure. Just as important are the relationships that an organization has externally.

The external relationships will be with either clients or suppliers of services of one sort or another. The client may be retail, corporate or institutional. They could be based in the same location or be remote and they could be overseas. The client profile is important for many business reasons and, of course, it is important for the type of service that will be provided. We deal with this subject in Chapter 5 so for the moment let us focus on the non-client relationships in the sense that we are in fact the client and utilize other organizations' services and facilities. By using Figure 3.1 we can see where these relationships might occur.

The various relationships that an organization might have will also be varied in their nature. In similar vein to internal relationships there will be those that are almost constant and others that are periodic. Some may be critical, others not so critical, and yet each is important in the overall scheme of things. We can look at some of these relationships from a specific point of view and consider the issues that arise for the Operations teams.

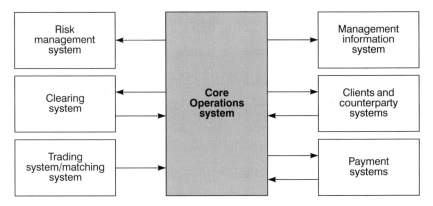

Figure 3.1 Operations relationships

Exchanges/markets

The obvious link between exchanges and Operations is the trans-action data. Today with more and more exchanges moving to electronic trading the links into the exchange's systems enables rapid access to trade data. As part of straight through processing projects, this link becomes vital enabling not only immediate sight of the transaction but also automated reconciliation. In some markets the link to the exchange system permits essential additional data to be added that will correctly route the trade to settlement. An example here would be the 'give-up' process in derivative exchanges where a trade executed by one member is routed for clearing and settlement to another member. Similarly, with securities the attaching of settlement instructions to a trade will help to ensure that it is settled on the due date. The ability to use such system links to the exchanges efficiently and correctly is therefore an integral part of the Operations process, but as automation of this trade data replaces the traditional trade manual process so the need to address resource issues arises. Figures 3.2 and 3.3 show two flows, one 'traditional' the other in an STP environment.

Now consider the resource and relationship issues that arise. In the STP environment there is obviously less manual intervention and so

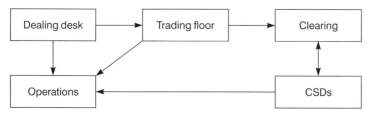

Figure 3.2 A 'traditional' flow

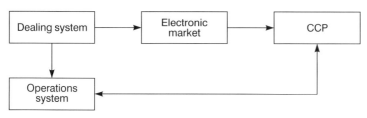

Figure 3.3 Flow in an STP environment

the process is quicker and there is a reduction in risk as well as an increased capacity to handle business. There is a danger that if any errors are not picked up or action taken to rectify them then there may be quite serious problems and so the resources on the Operations team are more concerned with dealing with exceptions and resolving problems than with inputting data. The main difference is this change of role for the personnel concerned and this is obviously an issue for the Operations manager, and particularly so if there are some markets that are fully electronic and part of an STP environment and other markets that are more manually handled. Procedures will be different and so too will the skill sets needed by the relevant individuals. What are the main differences?

The manual flow potentially needs a much higher degree of control and is more susceptible to fluctuating volumes, for example absence of staff. The time elapsed from the actual trade being executed to it being confirmed by Operations as being reconciled may be significant. Without the discipline of an electronic dealing system linked to an electronic exchange trading system that is accessed real-time by Operations there is always the possibility of an unidentified trade or an error. We know that a trade on an electronic market is matched but this does not mean that the trade executed is the one the dealer meant to undertake. A buy order can be entered to an in-house dealing system and/or an electronic exchange trading system just as easily as a sell order, so errors can and do occur. In markets where open-outcry trading exists there is the further problem of unmatched trades and the delay in getting the trade data into systems that can be accessed by Operations teams. This could be a matter of minutes or several hours.

Even when an in-house dealing system is in use there may be a delay in Operations receiving the data about trades. Look at Figure 3.4.

On some markets trade data is offered to the member through the system and if the Operations teams are waiting to confirm to the exchange that they accept the trade the timing and accuracy of the trade comparison is vital and so too is the speed of resolution of any discrepancies. Where this kind of arrangement is in existence it is not unheard of for exchanges to fine members that do not accept trades within a certain time period.

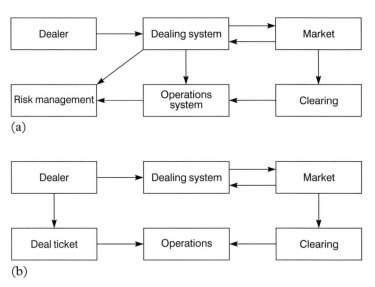

Figure 3.4 (a) Electronic flow of data; (b) Manual system (electronic market)

As well as trade data, Operations teams are relying on the exchange for other data needed for settlement or for static data on their own systems. This would include data such as:

- Prices for valuation purposes
- Data on corporate actions
- Changes to margin rates

This data may be published electronically or by hard-copy announcement or both. The Operations function relies considerably on correct static data so the resources employed in this area need to understand what data is needed, how often it changes, where and how it can be sourced and who is responsible for publishing it at the exchange.

Operations managers may also be involved in various committees and project teams looking at different aspects of the markets and how they might be improved or new products introduced. In recent years projects such as reducing the settlement cycle for equity securities have been a key undertaking for most markets and the involvement of Operations managers in deliberations on how and when to introduce new settlement conventions is critically important. However, it is not just shortening settlement cycles that demands a good relationship between exchange and member firms, many other equally important issues also need addressing and discussing. Without being part of the input to exchange projects the Operations managers and their organization are effectively being left out of crucial decisions that will affect them. A good Operations manager will seek to be a member of, or will ensure the team are members of, relevant industry committees.

Clearing houses

Operations teams have either direct or indirect relationships with the clearing houses for each market. As a direct clearing house member the key relationship and resource issues are:

- Meeting membership requirements
- Maintaining standards required by the clearing house
- Working with the clearing house to provide input to developments and projects being run by the clearing house

Clearing houses have specific requirements for potential members and these are both financial and operational. Within the central clearing counterpart arrangements there are conditions that are an obligation on the clearing member and any failure to meet that obligation will result in a default situation. It is vitally important therefore that in the relationship with the clearing house the Operations manager is aware of the procedures and processes for the clearing and settlement of transactions and also the obligations to which the organization is committing. In turn the manager must ensure that all the staff dealing or likely to be dealing with the clearing house also fully understand the obligations.

For instance, most clearing houses select their members on the basis of stringent regulatory and financial criteria in order to guarantee the market security. We can illustrate the obligations in more detail by looking at the following extract from the Clearnet Rule Book. Clearnet is the clearing organization for EURONEXT, an exchange that incorporates the markets of Belgium, France, Holland and Portugal as well as the London Financial Futures and Options Exchange, although the latter is currently cleared by the London Clearing House.

The extracts are very detailed but it is important to study them if we are to understand the obligations and issues that affect members and also what the Operations teams need to be aware of and deal with to meet the requirements. We can start by looking at what the Rule Book says about membership.

Clearnet rule book extracts

CHAPTER 4 – MEMBERSHIP

Section 1.4.1 ADMISSION OF CLEARING MEMBERS

A – STATUS

Article 1.4.1.1

A Clearing Member is a legal person admitted as such by Clearnet and authorised, subject to the Rules, to submit Transactions for registration, pursuant to an Admission Agreement between Clearnet and itself.

Article 1.4.1.2

The following entities are eligible to become a Clearing Member:
– Legal persons authorised to become members of Regulated Markets;
– Credit Institutions whose program of activity for clearing has been approved by their national Competent Authority or which are duly authorised by their Competent Authority to provide clearing activities;
– Legal persons, whose principal or sole object is the clearing of Financial Instruments, duly authorised by their national Competent Authority.

Such entities must be under their home country Competent Authority's supervision.

Article 1.4.1.3

A Clearing Member can operate as:

– Individual Clearing Member;
  or
– General Clearing Member.

The Admission Agreement specifies, *inter alia*, the Product Group and the membership category which the Clearing Member is authorised to clear.

B – APPLICATION PROCEDURE

Article 1.4.1.4

The items to be included in the admission application are specified in an Instruction.

The Admission Agreement is concluded on the basis of the identity of the relevant Clearing Member and so cannot be assigned or transferred without Clearnet's prior written approval.

Article 1.4.1.5

Clearnet shall examine the information in the admission application and inform the applicant of its admission decision by ordinary mail within one month following the date of receipt of all documents to be included in the application. Should the information contained in the application be incomplete or unsatisfactory, Clearnet shall have the right to require additional information from the applicant. The period within which the applicant must be informed of the decision of Clearnet shall run from the receipt of the complete admission application, including any additional information required by Clearnet.

Article 1.4.1.6

In the case of the approval of an application, Clearnet may impose conditions or limitations on the exercise of certain rights under these Rules provided that such conditions or limitations are imposed without discrimination.

Article 1.4.1.7

Whilst the application is pending, the Applicant must notify Clearnet in advance in writing of every change in the data supplied with the application and of facts and circumstances concerning the applicant which may be of importance in the context of the application or of the ability of the applicant to perform its obligations under the Rules and the orderly conduct of its activities as a Clearing Member.

Article 1.4.1.8

If Clearnet has not made a decision on a particular application within one month following the date on which the complete application was filed with Clearnet, Clearnet shall be deemed to have rejected the application.

Article 1.4.1.9

Clearnet may refuse an admission to membership if it considers that such admission may adversely affect the operation of the clearing and settlement system, or when the Applicant does not comply with its obligations resulting from its admission to another clearing house or Central Securities Depository.

On the request of the Applicant that was not admitted, Clearnet shall duly motivate its decision within one month after the request. Any Applicant facing a refusal decision from Clearnet is able to contest such decision before an appeal comity. The appeal procedure and the constitution of such comity are set out in an Instruction.

Article 1.4.1.10

If the Applicant has been approved as a Clearing Member, it shall before commencing operations:

– return the signed Admission Agreement signifying its acceptance of the Rules as a contracting party;
– pay to Clearnet its Admission Fee.

Article 1.4.1.11

A Clearing Member must commence operations within six months after admission, unless Clearnet grants an extension. Failing this, the admission decision shall be automatically revoked and any new admission will require compliance with the provisions of this Section.

Section 1.4.2 SPECIFIC REQUIREMENTS

A – ORGANISATIONAL REQUIREMENTS

Article 1.4.2.1

A General Clearing Member who clears Transactions for one or more Trading Members or Associated Trading Members must have signed a Clearing Agreement with each such Trading Member or Associated Trading Member.

The provisions which are required to be included in the Clearing Agreement are outlined in an Instruction and include provisions on the reciprocal obligations of the (Associated) Trading Member and the Clearing Member, the terms for Margin calls by the Clearing Member on the (Associated) Trading Member, the methods by which transactions are registered, the applicable law, and the procedure to be followed in the event of default of one of the signatories.

A General Clearing Member may only enter into a Clearing Agreement with an (Associated) Trading Member which has not yet entered into a Clearing Agreement with another General Clearing Member for that Product Group or for Financial Instruments traded on the same Euronext Market.

Article 1.4.2.2

The Clearing Agreement to be entered into by a General Clearing Member shall be submitted for prior approval to Clearnet.

If Clearnet deems changes or additions to the Clearing Agreement submitted to it appropriate, it will inform the General Clearing Member which shall make the required amendments. Clearnet may stipulate that approval of the Clearing Agreement is valid for a specific period only.

Article 1.4.2.3

Clearnet shall not be liable for any damage arising from the Clearing Agreement, whether sustained by the General Clearing Member or by a third party. The General Clearing Member shall comply with the Clearing Agreement as approved by Clearnet.

Any amendment to the provisions required by Clearnet to be included in the Clearing Agreement shall be subject to prior approval by Clearnet.

Article 1.4.2.4

Any Applicant wishing to be admitted as a Clearing Member by Clearnet should satisfy the following conditions:

(a) be validly incorporated;

(b) undertake to accept the Rules by executing the Admission Agreement;

(c) be the subject of supervision by its Competent Authorities, or of comparable local supervision, if the Applicant was incorporated outside the EEA;

(d) meet the financial requirements as determined by Clearnet from time to time and specified in Section 1.4.2, and also meet any further requirements as to liquidity and/or solvency as may be set by Clearnet;

(e) meet the quality requirements as specified in an Instruction;

(f) satisfy Clearnet that it has sufficient expertise in relation to clearing activities, that its technical systems and related organisational structure are operationally reliable and that its risk management policy is adequate;

(g) ensure that the persons who represent the Applicant fulfil the requirements of expertise and ability determined by Clearnet in Articles 1.4.2.6 to 1.4.2.8, and ensure that its organisation and the persons competent to take decisions will be accessible to Clearnet during working hours of every Clearing Day;

(h) submit details of duly existing accounts for the purposes of payment of cash amounts and deliveries of Financial Instruments, as well as evidence that a power of attorney has been issued in favour of Clearnet to allow the debiting or crediting of such accounts for the settlement of Transactions cleared by Clearnet;

(i) irrevocably authorise such persons as may be specified by Clearnet, to inspect its facilities, interview its staff, audit its Systems and Operations, check the proposed procedures (as recorded in writing) and inspect its books, papers and other data, for the purpose of determining whether the Rules are being properly complied with;

(j) satisfy such other requirements as may be imposed by Clearnet generally or for a category of Clearing Members.

Article 1.4.2.5

Applicants that are not established under the laws of France, Belgium or the Netherlands, or any other country that may be specified by Clearnet are obliged to provide Clearnet, at their earliest convenience, with all relevant information on rules and regulations that are in force in their Home State, which deal with clearing activities, and especially those rules and regulations that concern the registration of Transactions and the resolution of delivery fails between Clearing Members and their Clients.

B – AUTHORISED REPRESENTATIVES

Article 1.4.2.6

All individuals who wish to perform clearing functions on Regulated Markets under the authority or on behalf of a Clearing Member must be authorised by Clearnet. Clearnet grants such authorisation upon the terms and subject to the conditions specified in an Instruction.

Article 1.4.2.7

Before granting the authorisation, Clearnet will assess the applicant's professional knowledge and ability, if necessary by means of an examination.

Clearnet may revoke or suspend the authorisation in the circumstances specified in the Instruction referred to in Article 1.4.2.6.

Article 1.4.2.8

The Clearing Member shall provide Clearnet with a list of persons whose activities require such authorisation. Applications for authorisation are submitted by the Clearing Member, which is responsible for their proper submission.

Article 1.4.2.9

A Clearing Member cannot disavow the acts or omissions of any person acting or appearing to act on its behalf on the basis that such person was not duly authorised.

C – FINANCIAL REQUIREMENTS

Article 1.4.2.10

In order to clear Transactions dealt on a Regulated Market, an Individual Clearing Member must at all times maintain a Capital of at least EUR 10 million.

If the Clearing Member is not able to fulfil this requirement, a guarantee may be accepted in the conditions set forth below to cover the shortfall.

Article 1.4.2.11

An Individual Clearing Member with Capital between EUR 5 and EUR 10 million, must provide a Letter of Credit in favour of Clearnet to cover the shortfall, unless such Clearing Member can demonstrate, in a manner which is acceptable to Clearnet, a guarantee of one or more group company covering its obligations under these Rules.

In either case the identity of the issuer must be satisfactory to Clearnet. In the latter case, the form and substance of the guarantee must be satisfactory and the level of Capital is assessed on a consolidated basis.

Article 1.4.2.12

In order to clear Transactions dealt on a Regulated Market, a General Clearing Member must at all times maintain a Capital of at least EUR 25 million. The required amount increases, depending on the number of Trading Members cleared by the General Clearing Member, as follows:

EUR 30 million from the tenth Trading Member cleared,
EUR 33.75 million from the fifteenth Trading Member cleared,
EUR 37.5 million from the twentieth Trading Member cleared and above.

If the Clearing Member is not able to fulfil this requirement, a guarantee may be accepted in the conditions set forth below to cover the shortfall.

Article 1.4.2.13

A General Clearing Member with a Capital below the amounts stipulated in Article 1.4.2.12, but in excess of EUR 15 million, must provide a Letter of Credit in favour of Clearnet to cover the shortfall, unless such Clearing Member can demonstrate, in a manner which is acceptable to Clearnet, a guarantee of one or more group company covering its obligations under these Rules.

In either case the identity of the issuer must be satisfactory to Clearnet. In the latter case, the form and substance of the guarantee must be satisfactory and the level of Capital is assessed on a consolidated basis.

Article 1.4.2.14

The requirements set out in Sub-Section C of this Section shall also be applicable to Clearing Members clearing Prof Trades. Clearnet can also apply the provisions of this Section to the Members clearing Transactions in Financial Instruments executed on a market which does not have the status of Regulated Market if all Financial Instruments may be traded on that market are traded elsewhere on a Regulated Market.

Article 1.4.2.15

Any Letters of Credit that have been issued in favour of Clearnet to cover the obligations of another Clearing Member, pursuant to Articles 1.4.2.11 and 1.4.2.13, shall reduce the issuer's Capital pro tanto.

Article 1.4.2.16

In the case of Business Combinations, the minimum Capital shall be determined by adding the Capital of each Person in such combination which is jointly and severally liable, and subtracting any cross-share-holdings between such Persons. The total Capital must at all times be at least equivalent to the minimum amounts set forth in these Rules.

Article 1.4.2.17

A Clearing Member whose Capital at any point falls below the required amount is obliged to immediately ensure it is brought back up to the minimum requirement, without prejudice to the powers of Clearnet specified in Section 1.4.4.

D - LOCATION OF OFFICES

Article 1.4.2.18

A Clearing Member may locate the human and technical resources needed to carry on its clearing and back office activities wherever it chooses in the EEA, provided that it can satisfy Clearnet that such activities are carried out in a country in which on-site inspections by or on behalf of Clearnet are practicable and permitted by applicable laws and regulations. In any case, the head office and the registered office of the Clearing Member must be located in the same member state.

Article 1.4.2.19

A Clearing Member may subcontract all or part of its clearing activities, to another Clearing Member, or to a company in the same group with the prior authorisation of Clearnet, provided that such arrangements shall not relieve the subcontracting Clearing Member of any of its obligations under these Rules. The request for authorisation must give all appropriate details as to the organisation, structure and procedures of the subcontractor and as to the means of control and supervision available to the subcontracting Clearing Member.

Article 1.4.2.20

Clearnet may require from a subcontractor the same information as may be required from a Clearing Member pursuant to these Rules. To that effect Clearnet may require in advance a written undertaking by the subcontractor which will include a provision authorising Clearnet and any Person acting on its behalf to perform inspections at the premises in which the clearing activities actually take place.

Article 1.4.2.21

A Clearing Member that relies on an outside contractor to operate its information systems agrees to inform Clearnet of the control mechanisms pertaining to the hardware and software used or made available by the contractor. Such communications do not constitute approval by Clearnet; neither do they relieve the Clearing Member of any of its obligations under these Rules. The Clearing Member alone is answerable to Clearnet for the proper execution of operations.

Section 1.4.3 OTHER CONTINUING OBLIGATIONS

A – GENERAL

Article 1.4.3.1

Clearing Members shall at all times comply with the requirements set out in Section 1.4.2 and any additional conditions and limitations imposed upon admission and with any other stipulation of these Rules.

In particular, they must pay any Clearing Fees and contribute to the Clearing Fund as set forth in Chapter 6 of this Title.

Article 1.4.3.2

Clearing Members must ensure that they are able to effect the settlement of Financial Instruments irrespective of the currency in which they are settled.

Article 1.4.3.3

Clearnet may furnish, within the limits of the legal provisions applicable, any information provided to it to exchanges, clearing organisations and Competent Authorities to the extent that these exchanges, clearing organisations and Competent Authorities are responsible for the organisation of markets, the clearing, settlement or the supervision of other activities of Clearing Members. Before furnishing the information, Clearnet may require that the exchange, clearing organisation or Competent Authorities concerned confirms that the information will be treated in confidence and that it will not be used for any purpose other than that for which it has been furnished. Notwithstanding such confirmation, the exchange, clearing organisation or Competent Authorities concerned shall have the right to provide the information furnished by Clearnet to third parties if it is legally empowered or obliged to do so.

B – INFORMATION

Article 1.4.3.4

The Clearing Member shall respond to all requests for information from Clearnet concerning its clearing activities and exposure to general and financial risks (Transactions, positions, fails, Clients, etc.).

B 1 – Financial information

Article 1.4.3.5
Clearing Members must send the following information to Clearnet:
- Annually:
  - audited financial statements – balance sheet, profit and loss account, and notes to the annual financial statements;
  - audited consolidated financial statements – balance sheet, profit and loss account, and notes to the financial statements;
- At the intervals required by the Competent Authority or by the regulations of the Home State:
  - interim balance sheet;
  - profit and loss account;
  - documents concerning prudential supervision of market risks, prepared on a consolidated or unconsolidated basis,
  - statements concerning core capital (tier 1) and supplementary capital (tier 2) as defined by the said authority or regulations.

Article 1.4.3.6
Clearing Members shall send Clearnet an annual update to a questionnaire relating to, inter alia:
  - the ownership of the Clearing Member's Capital, and a group organisation chart, an updated description of the technical resources and personnel that are assigned to clearing functions,
  - a description of the structure and procedures in place, particularly in regard to the audit and back office functions.

B 2 – Complementary information

Article 1.4.3.7
A Clearing Member must notify Clearnet in advance in writing of every change in the data supplied in its application for admission and of any facts and circumstances concerning the Clearing Member which may significantly affect the exercise of its duties or the orderly conduct of its activities as a Clearing Member. Such developments without limitation include in particular:

- those which could or are likely to result in the Clearing Member no longer being able to comply with its obligations under these Clearing Rules,
- any significant change in its financial situation, in particular where shareholders' equity or Letters of Credit have declined by more than 10% compared with the amounts previously reported or if shareholders' equity and Letters of Credit fall below the amount specified in Sub-Section C of Section 1.4.2 of these Rules,
- any other change which has or could have a significant impact on their financial position, reliability or operations,
- any change in their legal status or structure, including change of address, office or object under their Articles of Association,
- changes in the power of control (shareholders) over their business with respect to the appointment and dismissal of their personnel, changes in the composition of their management or executive bodies, in their accounting system or organisation, in the holders of a qualified participating interest in their business, in the participating interests they hold or the joint ventures or alliances they have entered into,
- any event occurring between the reporting dates set out in Article 1.4.3.6 that would significantly reduce the Clearing Members' Capital.

The obligation to notify becomes effective at the time the Clearing Member anticipates or becomes aware of the events, or, if earlier, at the time at which the Clearing Member ought reasonably to have anticipated or become so aware.

Article 1.4.3.8
Clearing Members shall send Clearnet a copy of all injunctions, formal notifications or sanctions imposed on it by any Competent Authority.

Article 1.4.3.9
The obligation of Clearing Members to provide information also covers information about their Clients, including personal particulars concerning the identity, trading activities and positions of Clients. Clearnet shall have the right to furnish this information to the same persons as mentioned in Article 1.4.3.3 and on the same terms.

C – RECORD KEEPING

Article 1.4.3.10

Clearing Members must keep accurate and full accounting records of all the Transactions they have entered into. These accounting records should, where applicable, disclose at least the following particulars:

– the Trading Member on the relevant market with which a Clearing Agreement has been entered into;
– in respect of each Trading Member on the relevant market with which a Clearing Agreement has been entered into, all the rights and obligations arising from the Transactions entered into by a General Clearing Member for the account of the Trading Member concerned;
– any further requirements as may be specified by Clearnet.

Article 1.4.3.11

The Clearing Member is required to keep all data relating to its clearing activity for at least five years and must make the data available to Clearnet upon demand throughout that period.

D – INVESTIGATION

Article 1.4.3.12

The Clearing Member authorises Clearnet to request all relevant information regarding its payment–delivery commitments in the payment and settlement systems used by Clearnet, either directly or through another organisation.

Article 1.4.3.13

The Clearing Member agrees to submit to inspections by Clearnet, whether on the latter's initiative or at the request of a national Competent Authority, and to respond to all requests by Clearnet for information on a regular or exceptional basis.

Article 1.4.3.14

The Clearing Member authorises Clearnet, or any person or entity that has been duly designated, to make an audit of its Systems and Operations.

Further, it undertakes to provide all information needed to complete such an audit. Clearnet reserves the right, upon completion of the audit, to require any modifications that may prove necessary. The Clearing Member hereby agrees to implement such modifications as soon as possible.

Article 1.4.3.15
For the purpose of this Clearing Rule Book, Clearnet may delegate its investigation powers to any suitable body which it shall see fit.

Section 1.4.4 SUSPENSION REVOCATION

Article 1.4.4.1
Without prejudice to the possible applicability of the provisions set out in Chapter 7 of this Title 1, if Clearnet is of the opinion that specific developments could or are likely to result in a situation in which a Clearing Member no longer satisfies one or more of the requirements set in Section 1.4.2, or endangers the proper functioning of the clearing system, or can no longer comply with its obligations under these Rules, Clearnet may:

- suspend or revoke its membership,
- refuse to register Transactions,
- submit registration of Transactions to specific conditions, or impose additional conditions which Clearnet deems appropriate in the circumstances and notifies in writing to the Clearing Member.

Article 1.4.4.2
Before exercising any such power, however, Clearnet may, without any commitment on its part, enter into consultations with the Clearing Member, which may result in Clearnet specifying the latest date and time limit on which the Clearing Member must have remedied the situation.

Article 1.4.4.3
In any event, Clearnet can decide the temporary suspension of the Clearing Member's activities, or revoke its membership as a Clearing

Member, with immediate effect without any further act or notification being required.

Article 1.4.4.4

When a Clearing Member's membership is suspended, Clearnet shall suspend the registration of any new Transactions in the Clearing Member's name. However, Clearnet may decide, in view of the particular circumstances to only suspend the registration of a new Transaction increasing the Clearing Member's Open Position. The Clearing Member will continue to be required to provide Collateral and settle netted Open Positions as they fall due.

Article 1.4.4.5

When a Clearing Member's membership is revoked, Clearnet shall discontinue registration of any new Transactions in the Clearing Member's name and transfer to another Clearing Member or liquidate the Clearing Member's Open Position(s).

Article 1.4.4.6

Suspension or revocation of membership shall be promptly notified to the Clearing Members by publication in a Clearnet Notice. Clearnet will also promptly notify the Competent Authorities and the operator of the markets concerned.

Article 1.4.4.7

In addition to the foregoing, Clearnet shall have the right at any time to terminate in writing a Clearing Member's membership, subject to a period of notice which is reasonable in the circumstances. The Clearing Member will be informed of the reason for the termination.

Section 1.4.5 WITHDRAWAL

Article 1.4.5.1

A Clearing Member shall have the right at all times to terminate its membership as a Clearing Member as specified in the Admission Agreement.

Article 1.4.5.2

The announcement of termination of membership does not relieve a Clearing Member from any of its obligations arising from Transactions entered into prior to such announcement. When the Clearing Member shall have satisfied all of his obligations vis-à-vis Clearnet, the latter will refund any remaining cash and Collateral belonging to the Clearing Member in question, including its contribution to the Clearing Fund.

Section 1.4.6 TRANSITIONAL PROVISIONS

A – GRAND FATHER CLAUSE

Article 1.4.6.1

As of the Transfer Date, all Clearing Members of BXS Clearing, AEX – Effectenclearing and AEX – Optieclearing, duly authorised at that time are automatically admitted to membership of Clearnet as Individual or General Clearing Member, in the relevant Product Group(s). For that purpose, they have to sign an appropriate Admission Agreement with Clearnet.

At the same time Clearnet becomes automatically the central counter-party of all the Open Positions of such Clearing Members and the beneficiary of all associated Collateral.

Article 1.4.6.2

As of the Transfer Date, upon notification as provided below, Clearnet will automatically grant an authorisation to all individuals, duly authorised at that date by BXS Clearing, AEX – Effectenclearing and AEX – Optieclearing, carrying out clearing functions for Clearing Members, subject only to the relevant Clearing Members notifying Clearnet the names of individuals concerned by this provision within 3 months after the Transfer Date.

B – TRANSITION PERIOD

Article 1.4.6.3

From the Transfer Date until December 31st, 2002, existing Clearing Members which do not meet the status, the organisational or financial requirements as set out in these Rules, are allowed to carry on their business exclusively for the clearing of Financial Instruments that they have been authorised previously, on the basis set out below.

Article 1.4.6.4

Any such Clearing Member, which wants to carry on its clearing business after the Implementation Date, must commit to fulfilling the financial requirements set out in Sub-Section C of Section 1.4.2 of this Clearing Rule Book before December 31st, 2002 at the latest.

For that purpose it will submit to Clearnet for approval a financial forecast to show how it will be able to meet the financial requirements. This forecast must be submitted to Clearnet as soon as possible after the Transfer Date and not later than the Implementation Date. An Instruction sets out the main criteria which Clearnet will take into account to approve or not such forecast.

Article 1.4.6.5

If Clearnet approves the financial forecast, the Clearing Member is automatically authorised, at the Implementation Date, to clear all Transactions executed on any Euronext Markets.

Article 1.4.6.6

After the approval of the forecast by Clearnet, and as long as the Clearing Member's Capital is still below the level which would otherwise be required, the Clearing Member shall report its Capital to Clearnet on a quarterly basis and have to cover its risks by:

– either providing Clearnet with a Letter of Credit covering the amount which Clearnet deems appropriate,

or

– paying an 'extra individualised margin' which should equal the difference between the calculated margin and a stress calculated margin. The stress calculation should be determined once a month, based on the highest risk exposure of the previous month. The extra individualised margin should be maximised with the difference between the required level of Capital and the present Capital of that Clearing Member.

Article 1.4.6.7

If Clearnet does not approve the financial forecast, or if the Clearing Member considers that it will not be able to fulfil the financial requirement set out in Sub-Section C of Section 1.4.2 of this Clearing Rule Book at the latest on December 31st, 2002, or if the Clearing Member fails to perform in accordance to the forecast, Clearnet may revoke the membership.

All the Open Positions and associated Collateral of such Clearing Member, will be transferred at the same time to a General Clearing Member designated by such Clearing Member.

Article 1.4.6.8

From Transfer Date until they fulfil the financial requirements set out in these Rules, the Clearing Members must comply either with the financial requirements defined in the Local Parts or with the financial requirements that were in force at December 31st, 2000 and that were applicable to the membership category they belonged to at the same date.

Clearing Members that satisfy the financial requirements set out in Sub-Section C of Section 1.4.2 of this Clearing Rule Book, either at the effective date of this Clearing Rule Book or in due course, must continuously observe the new obligations defined above.

Article 1.4.6.9

As of January 1st, 2003 all Clearing Members have to comply with the above mentioned status, organisational and financial requirements.

We can see from these requirements just how detailed the requirements for membership of the clearing house is. This is an enormously important issue for the operations manager as the Article 1.4.6.9 above indicates, because by January 1st, 2003 all Clearing Members previously with the clearing houses of the merged markets must be in compliance.

There are other very important requirements that personnel working in the clearing member firm must understand like keeping records for five years or that Clearnet may authorise an audit of the members' systems. The organisational requirements also make it essential that the manager has adequate procedures in place and that the staff fully understand the requirements.

Chapter 5 of the Rule Book looks at margin and again there are important requirements on the member.

CHAPTER 5 – MARGIN REQUIREMENTS AND RISK SUPERVISION

Section 1.5.1 MARGIN

Article 1.5.1.1
Initial Margins as well as Variation Margins are called to protect Clearnet against Clearing Member default.

Article 1.5.1.2
Variation Margin is debited or credited by Clearnet on a daily frequency.

Article 1.5.1.3
Based on the Open Positions of Clearing Members at any time during the day, Clearnet shall have the right during the day to re-determine or to call Margin upon Clearing Members and to inform them accordingly. If this results in a higher Margin, the Clearing Member in question shall be obliged to ensure that the difference between the previous Margin and the newly determined Margin is transferred or, as the case may be issued, within one hour of it having been informed thereof.

Article 1.5.1.4
Clearnet shall at all times have the right to impose upon a Clearing Member such additional Margin as it reasonably deems useful or necessary. This can be done either on an individual basis or based on the

nature of the Financial Instruments to which the relevant positions relate.

Article 1.5.1.5

Clearnet shall publish in an Instruction:

- the method and parameters used to calculate Initial Margin,
- any price fluctuation limits,
- the type of Securities, assets or bank guarantees to be accepted as Collateral to meet Initial Margin or Variation Margin calls by Clearnet and by Clearing Members,
- any discount ('haircut') to be applied to the market value of such Collateral, depending on its nature and maturity.

Article 1.5.1.6

Clearing Members shall call Margin from their Clients and Trading Members having positions on Derivatives in an amount based on the same parameters and methodology as the Clearnet Margin.

For Transactions on Securities Markets, the provisions concerning Margin on Securities Positions are set forth in the Local Parts.

Section 1.5.2 COLLATERAL

Article 1.5.2.1

A Clearing Member shall provide sufficient Collateral to Clearnet or via a cross guarantee arranged with a central bank as security for the performance of the obligations of the Clearing Member. The amount of Collateral is determined by Clearnet.

Article 1.5.2.2

Any Margin required to be provided by a Clearing Member must be provided not later than the time set by Clearnet, on the Clearing Day following the day of the Transaction.

Where the Clearing Member is to provide Collateral in the form of the issuance of a guarantee by a central bank, it must fulfil its obligation to provide eligible Collateral to the central bank by the time stipulated in the relevant guarantee agreement so that the central bank can issue its guarantee to Clearnet by the same time as specified above.

Article 1.5.2.3

Where Collateral is due to Clearnet, Clearnet reserves the right to exclude certain types of Collateral on the grounds, *inter alia*, of illiquidity or insufficient outstandings, and may accept other assets on the terms specified by Clearnet in a Notice.

Section 1.5.3 RISK SUPERVISION AND ACCOUNTING

Article 1.5.3.1

At Clearnet's request, Clearing Members shall communicate to Clearnet all information concerning the identity, the positions, and the solvency of the Clients whose accounts they hold.

Article 1.5.3.2

Clearnet can request daily information of the Clearing Member in order to continuously monitor the risk management as performed by the Clearing Member.

Article 1.5.3.3

Clearnet shall keep accounting records of the positions of all Clearing Members concerning the Financial Instruments they are due to receive and deliver and of the related rights and obligations, by means of an account which Clearnet opens in its books in the name of each Clearing Member. The minimum requirement of the account structure at Clearnet level are set out in the respective Local Part until the Implementation Date.

Article 1.5.3.4

Clearnet requires Clearing Members to open position sub-accounts, in order to separately record the positions of Trading Members and those of the Clearing Member's Clients under the conditions set out in an Instruction.

Article 1.5.3.5

Position limits and limits on risk exposure applicable to Clearing Members and Clients are set out in an Instruction.

Article 1.5.3.6

When these limits are reached, Clearnet may refuse to register any Transaction which would increase the Open Position of the Clearing Member, Trading Member or the Client, after informing the operators of the market or Designated Clearnet Gateways. Clearnet can also increase the Collateral requirement in respect of the Clearing Member's or the Client's Open Positions.

Article 1.5.3.7

In addition, Clearnet may order a Clearing Member to reduce its own, its Clients or Trading Members Open Position within a stipulated time limit. If the Open Position is not reduced within the time limit, Clearnet can automatically liquidate the Open Positions of the Clearing Member(s) that exceed the authorised limits. Further, Clearnet can also establish a market position limit and can require that, from a specified date onwards, only closing orders will be accepted.

The margin requirements on the member cover such issues as separate accounts for the firm's principal and client positions, exposures and how and when margin can be called. If these obligations are not met then a default can occur. When defaults occur the clearing house utilizes a clearing fund. Again there are important requirements and issues for the member as we can see by looking at Chapters 6 and 7 of the Rule Book.

CHAPTER 6 – CLEARING FUND

Section 1.6.1 CONTRIBUTION TO THE FUND

Article 1.6.1.1
A Clearing Member is obliged to contribute to the Clearing Fund:

- by providing to Clearnet in a form approved by Clearnet either by means of Letter of Credit or outright transfer of Collateral,
- or by transferring Collateral to a central bank as Collateral for the issuance of a guarantee in favour of Clearnet,
- by any other means identified in the Local Parts or published in an Instruction.

In the second case, the Clearing Member must ensure the performance of the central bank's obligations by entering into arrangements acceptable to Clearnet for the issuance of such guarantees.

Article 1.6.1.2
The amount to be contributed by a Clearing Member to the Clearing Fund shall be correlated with the risk associated with the Open Positions (uncovered risk).

Article 1.6.1.3
Once a month Clearnet shall determine the size of the Clearing Fund and the level of each individual Clearing Member's contribution. The total amount that may initially be called shall at least cover the price risk run by the Clearing Member in respect of its largest uncovered risk. The method of calculation of such contribution is specified in an Instruction.

Section 1.6.2 CALLS UPON THE FUND

Article 1.6.2.1
Calls may be made on the Clearing Fund in the event that a Clearing Member is declared by Clearnet in default in order to cover the defaulting Members' obligations under these Rules.

Article 1.6.2.2
The defaulting Clearing Member's share in the Clearing Fund shall be used in the first instance.

Article 1.6.2.3
If a need remains thereafter, the other Clearing Member's shares in the Clearing Fund shall be used pro rata to their respective contributions for that monthly period. The Clearing Member's contribution thus calculated shall not exceed the total Clearing Fund contribution set for that period.

Article 1.6.2.4
Following a call, funds received from a central bank pursuant to any guarantees issued in favour of Clearnet as provided in Article 1.6.1.1 shall provide a valid discharge of the amount owed by the respective Clearing Members.

Article 1.6.2.5
If Clearnet calls upon the Clearing Fund, it shall use the sums provided to perform its obligations pursuant to its guarantee under Section 1.3.6 and any related loans, expenses, damages, interest charges and other expenditure.

Article 1.6.2.6
Should there be any surplus after such performance, or profits earned from the performance of its obligations, then such amounts shall be repaid by Clearnet to Clearing Members in proportion to their respective contributions either directly, or where applicable, via the central bank.

Section 1.6.3 FURTHER CONTRIBUTIONS

Article 1.6.3.1
If a Clearing Member is declared in default under the Rules and a call has been made on the Clearing Fund, each Clearing Member (including the Clearing Member in default) shall be required to contribute further to the Clearing Fund to restore their contributions and raise the Clearing Fund to the required level in such time as notified by Clearnet. Following that,

Clearnet shall not be allowed to make further calls on the Clearing Fund in respect of the same default.

Article 1.6.3.2
Payment of the amounts referred to in this Chapter shall not affect the obligation of the defaulting Clearing Member to properly perform its obligations and pay compensation for any damage caused by its default.

Article 1.6.3.3
From time to time, Clearnet will report on and account for any withdrawals made from the Clearing Fund.

Article 1.6.3.4
The Clearing Fund described in this Chapter shall be segregated to the effect that there will exist two separate Dutch Clearing Funds as described in Title 2 on the one hand, and a separate Clearing Fund for Belgian and French Clearing Members on the other hand, until a date that will be published in a Notice and no later than the end of the Transition Period.

CHAPTER 7 – EVENT OF DEFAULT – LIABILITY – FORCE MAJEURE

Article 1.7.0.1
In the interests of the clearing system, Clearnet may, in co-ordination with the Competent Authority, take any measure it deems necessary in relation to the organisation and the operation of the clearing and settlement system, whether or not these measures are set out in the Rules.

Section 1.7.1 DEFINITION OF DEFAULT

Article 1.7.1.1
If the Clearing Member appears to Clearnet to be unable, or to be likely to become unable, to meet its obligations in respect of one or more

Transactions or otherwise under the Rules, Clearnet declares such event as an event of default.

Clearnet may take the view that an event of default has happened in the light of the occurrence of *inter alia* any of the following events:

- Failure to pay or deliver any or all balances, Financial Instruments, or assets owed to Clearnet in respect of Open Positions registered in the name of the Clearing Member with Clearnet, within the stipulated deadlines,
- Failure to pay Initial Margin, Variation Margin or any additional Margin *as indicated in Article 1.5.1.4*, imposed by Clearnet or failure to make a required contribution to the Clearing Fund, within the stipulated time limits,
- Being subject to a suspension of payments, bankruptcy, administration or amicable settlement, or similar proceedings (excluding attachment procedures).

Section 1.7.2 MEASURES IN CASE OF A DEFAULT

Article 1.7.2.1

Upon the occurrence of an event of default, Clearnet, without any notification being required, may declare the Clearing Member in default and/or take any measures that may be needed or useful for the protection of the clearing system, in particular any one or more of the following, or any other measure as may be provided elsewhere in the Rule Book or Admission Agreement:

(i)   to refuse to register any new Transactions in the Clearing Member's name or to agree to register only under specific conditions if, in the opinion of Clearnet, there are good reasons for this;

(ii)   to require Clearnet's authorisation for the registration of any new Transaction in the Clearing Member's name;

(iii) to demand compliance by the Clearing Member of its obligations in the manner as determined by Clearnet;

(iv) to impose further requirements as regards Collateral to be furnished to secure the Clearing Member's compliance with its obligations;

(v) to claim damages and costs;

(vi) to declare one or more of the obligations of the Clearing Member to be due and payable immediately;

(vii) to buy, borrow or sell Securities for the account of the Clearing Member to secure compliance with the Settlement obligations of the Clearing Member;

(viii) in compliance with the obligations of the Clearing Member under these Rules to sell off the Collateral furnished by the Clearing Member;

(ix) to effect cash settlement of any Open Positions in the name of the defaulting Clearing Member;

(x) to express the obligations of the Clearing Member or Clearnet, as the case may be, in money to be valued at the Settlement Price of that day and to set off reciprocal balances so that these obligations, in so far as set off, will have been met;

(xi) to liquidate some or all of the Transactions registered in the Clearing Member's own account and that of companies in its corporate group;

(xii) to liquidate the Open Positions of Clients or Trading Members which cannot or do not wish to maintain their positions with the new Clearing Member;

(xiii) to transfer to another Clearing Member designated by the beneficiary the Open Positions, including positions of its Clients or Trading Members;

(xiv) to act in lieu of the defaulting Clearing Member to pay funds and deliver Securities due;

(xv) to obtain any advice or assistance, as Clearnet may reasonably require in connection with the default at the expense of the defaulting Clearing Member;

(xvi) to impose a penalty for late delivery or payment, in the circumstances and a rate set out in an Instruction.

Section 1.7.3 LIABILITY OF CLEARING MEMBERS

Article 1.7.3.1
The Clearing Member shall be liable for any damage which Clearnet suffers directly or indirectly as a consequence of event of default without any notice of default by Clearnet being required.

Article 1.7.3.2
All expenses incurred by Clearnet to process the default shall be deducted from the Margins of the defaulting Clearing Member or where relevant any other funds deposited by such Member with Clearnet. Any remaining balance shall be remitted to the Clearing Member after Clearnet has discharged all its obligations.

Article 1.7.3.3
If the defaulting buying Clearing Member's Open Positions are liquidated, any excess Collateral is refunded to the defaulting buying Clearing Member only once the following conditions are met:

- Clearnet has paid the selling Clearing Member;
- Clearnet has closed out the buying Clearing Member's Open Positions and has calculated all costs, including *inter alia* the Transaction costs.

Any profit on the sale of the Securities received from the selling Clearing Member is applied against amounts payable to Clearnet.

Article 1.7.3.4
The balance of the regular Margin and additional Margin called – after allocation of the results of the Securities buy-in and any costs incurred in processing the default – is refunded to the defaulting selling Clearing Member only once the following conditions are met:

- The buying Clearing Member has either taken delivery or has received the cash settlement in lieu of delivery,

– Clearnet has calculated all costs, in particular, that Clearnet has no outstanding borrowings related to its settlement of the default.

Any profit on the buy-in and delivery of Securities to the Clearing Member buyer is applied against amounts payable to Clearnet.

Section 1.7.4 LIABILITY OF CLEARNET FORCE MAJEURE

Article 1.7.4.1
In no circumstance shall Clearnet incur any liability for any breach of the Rules by a Clearing Member.

Article 1.7.4.2
The Clearing Member buyer's Open Position is no longer carried in clearing once he has received delivery of Securities tendered either by Clearnet or the Clearing Member seller. The Clearing Member buyer can assert no claim to compensation for the late receipt of Securities.

Article 1.7.4.3
Clearnet shall be liable for damage arising from non-compliance with its delivery or payment obligation under Transactions it has entered into with Clearing Members unless such non-compliance is the result of a *force majeure* event.

Article 1.7.4.4
Force majeure is to be given its construction under French law, that is to say extraordinary events independent of the Parties' will that cannot be foreseen or avoided by them even with due diligence, being beyond their control preventing the Parties to comply with their obligations undertaken in these Rules or in the Admission Agreement.

Disasters, such as hurricane, earthquake, international conflicts, stroke of lightning and war, are *inter alia* to be considered as such events.

If circumstances as referred to in the previous paragraph occur or are in danger of occurring, Clearnet or Clearing Members, as the case may be, will take such measures as may be reasonably demanded of them in order to limit as much as possible the detrimental consequences for the other party resulting from these circumstances.

Article 1.7.4.5
For damage arising from obligations other than those referred to in Article 1.7.4.4 above, Clearnet will under no circumstances be held liable unless such damage is a direct result of gross negligence or an intentional act or omission on the part of Clearnet.

Article 1.7.4.6
Clearnet will not be held liable for any detrimental consequences of abnormal or fraudulent use of the clearing system or for any detrimental consequences of acts or omissions of third parties.

Clearnet will under no circumstances be liable for consequential loss suffered by the Clearing Member such as loss of custom, profit or revenues believed by the Clearing Member to be the consequence of a total or partial failure to perform the Rules or the Admission Agreement.

Source: Clearnet SA website

From studying these extracts from the Clearnet Rule Book we clearly see how the member firm has entered into a relationship where there are significant issues and requirements for both the clearing house and the clearing member. There are obligations, operational requirements and liabilities. There are also actions the clearing house can take if these conditions are not satisfactorily met by the member.

Given this, we can see why some organizations prefer or indeed are forced to be non-clearing members.

Clearnet is a central clearing counterparty but not all markets have clearing houses that settle in this way. Some act as a conduit for matching processes and settlement instructions. This involves no actual settlement by the clearing house and instead the transactions settle by acting on instructions to securities depositories, banks and custodians.

Custodians, depositories, banks and payment systems

Most settlement requires the exchange of cash for assets. Therefore the organizations that hold and move assets and cash become vital counterparties and relationships for those operating in the financial markets. The interaction of these organizations is crucial to efficient and safe settlement of business in all the markets. Central securities depositories and custodians came about to help reduce the loss of valuable securities and the time it took to transfer ownership of securities.

The relationship between the clients of banks, custodians and depositories will, of course, be slightly different in each case although primarily they are each providing services. Membership of payment systems will place responsibilities on treasury operations managers to ensure that they have adequately trained staff and also that they have understood and incorporated into the procedures all the requirements, processes and procedures associated with the particular payment system.

SWIFT, the Society For Worldwide Interbank Financial Transactions, is one of the most important organizations in the clearing and settlement processes, its 7000 members in approximately 200 countries exchanging millions of messages related to payments, securities, etc. daily. The SWIFT corporate message states:

SWIFT is a worldwide community of financial institutions whose

purpose is to be the leader in communications solutions enabling

interoperability between its members, their market infrastructures

and their end-user communities.

SWIFT will:

− *Work in partnership with its members to provide low-cost, competitive financial processing and communication services of the highest security and reliability.*

− *Contribute significantly to the commercial success of its members through greater automation of the end-to-end financial transaction process, based on its leading expertise in message processing and financial standards setting.*

− *Capitalise on its position as an international open forum for the world's financial institutions to address industry-level threats, issues and opportunities.*

− *Employ and recruit the best people, invest in the most beneficial resources, and become a leading global organisation respected for its professionalism, effectiveness, vision and management.*

Source: SWIFT website

Clearly being a member of SWIFT would be based on both commercial issues such as the ability to send messages and communicate with counterparties quickly, efficiently and reliably, but also it would be a relationship that enabled the member to participate in a leading forum in the industry. A similar situation arises with proprietary systems used by depositories and custodians and with membership of industry organizations such as the International Securities Services Association.

As we saw with Clearnet, most relationships with external organiza-tions such as clearing houses, custodians, depositories and payment systems involve meeting their requirements as well as being a client and receiving high-quality services. This would be true also of fund administrators and prime brokers and we look at those organizations in greater detail in Chapter 5 and also of system suppliers, which we cover in the next chapter.

How do we summarize the responsibilities, issues and problems that the Operations manager faces in dealing with external relationships and resourcing?

The first thing to bear in mind is that we have in many cases this dual situation of complying with requirements and receiving services. The benefits we expect to receive from the services must be measured against the requirements we must comply with. For instance, appointing a new custodian may appear a solution to poor service from the incumbent but what are the logistics of moving to a new counterparty?

Retraining, new system interfaces, transfer of assets, new instructions and mandates, etc. will be needed. Operational risk will increase temporarily and the new relationship will take time to settle down. Were the problems so insurmountable that this course of action was the only viable one? Equally, being a member of a central clearing counterparty has many advantages but there will be onerous requirements on the Operations team and we must be convinced we have the adequate and properly trained staff to meet the requirements. If we fail to pay attention to the level of standards required by the clearing house, payment system or depository, we may end up having our membership revoked or suspended, neither of which is going to be well received by senior management or our clients and counterparties!

Managing the relationships

Managing the relationships is all about the ability to identify the deliverables on both sides and to monitor the delivery of the requirements. Allied to this is the ability to manage problems constructively.

One source of problems in any relationship is people and this is looked at in Chapter 4. Another contribution is the understanding of the product or service offered/used and the competency of the people involved in the processes. An excellent processor who is highly experienced may not have the personality to be able to deal with clients.

Clearly, personalities play a part and the manager must approach relationship management as the basis of marrying the skills and experience with the right person so that whoever is leading the relationship with the external party will be respected and liked.

Service suppliers and agents will have service level agreements and so in this respect the Operations manager must ensure that the agreement contains sufficient details of the deliverables.

Most day-to-day problems that occur are routine and easily dealt with. The key concerns must be repetitive problems and situations when the service levels and/or the relationship begin to deteriorate. The causes must be identified quickly before the problems escalate and become difficult to resolve and possibly irreparable. Good quality management information is crucial in helping to identify the problems, as are periodic review meetings with peer groups internally (to assess the relationship across the firm) and at the counterparty.

External relationships will affect the performance of the Operations team and they must be viewed as a two-way partnership that will be of benefit to the function. Poorly performing counterparties need to be made aware of the problems they are causing and if no improvement occurs the possibility of change must be considered. Once the firm's own performance is being affected there are operational risk, reputation and profitability issues that will arise and simply cannot be ignored. Deciding on the external counterparty,

where there is a choice, and managing the relationship are fundamental roles for managers and supervisors. If they get it wrong the
consequences can be quite severe.

In the end, relationship management is as good as the communication and information flow about the relationship. Good managers
make a point of monitoring the various relationships and ensuring
that any problems are noted and dealt with efficiently and in a timely
way.

Chapter 4

The Operations team – managing systems and people

Introduction

The management of people and systems is a key function of the managers and supervisors. The objectives for successful management are broadly driven by consideration in respect of:

- Risk management
- Efficiency
- Cost effectiveness
- Competitive advantage
- Developing and implementing procedures
- Control
- Compliance with regulation and controls
- Business development
- Continuity and development of staff
- Provision of client services
- Record keeping

As a result the demands on managers and supervisors are considerable. Today the role has been expanded and as well as operational issues such as processes and procedures, we now have skills requirements in the client-facing and risk-management areas. We can also add to this an involvement in profit generation and protection so that preventing unnecessary errors and costs becomes a key driver.

With such a change in the role and a situation where significant change is also occurring in the industry in all sorts of ways, the manager's role in ensuring that systems are capable of handling the current and future business and that the team is being trained and retrained to meet the new environment, is, to say the least, demanding. This chapter looks at these functions and roles.

Managing systems

Systems are crucial to derivative operations. The effectiveness of systems depends on both the suitability of the system for the business being undertaken and the capability of managers and supervisors to utilize the system. It is also essential that the systems are recognized as key risk components being vulnerable to both failure and security risk.

The interaction between people and systems is at the heart of the operation. Links to various sources of information as well as users accessing the systems will be a key factor in the effectiveness and efficiency of the operation in general and impacts significantly on areas such as:

- Client-facing products and services
- Group risk management
- STP

The robustness of systems is a key regulatory requirement, it is also a key internal risk matter.

One only needs to look at cases where system failures have precipitated dire consequences for organizations. Brokerage businesses have ceased functioning because of the inability to meet the regulatory competency levels for settlement of transactions. Failures in control over static data, system access and input and amendment of data have generated high-profile 'disasters'.

Consider the following extract from the *FOA Guidelines for End-users of Derivatives*, published in 1995 yet still a fundamental concept today:

> *Systems Approval*
>
> *Computer systems used for recording derivative transactions should be subject to the same procedures and controls as for other systems used by the organization (including contingency plans and back up). In particular, the pricing models and trade recording systems should be properly controlled to ensure that only authorized amendments or overrides are made. Derivative systems should be reviewed to ensure that they integrate properly into the organization's normal reporting systems, that they are sufficiently robust to be able to continue to operate as the number of transactions increases and that they comply with any applicable regulatory requirements.*

Figure 4.1 shows some of the generic links between systems. It is obvious that many processes and instructions move data between these systems every day. All this data is critical and the robustness factor means that no weak link can exist in the chain without serious implications for quality, reliability and risk control.

Given this importance of the systems, which cannot be over-emphasized, there are significant questions for managers to answer:

- What are the objectives for the systems employed?
- How is the effectiveness of systems measured?
- What are the resource and skill sets needed for support?
- What are the contingency plans that are needed against failures?

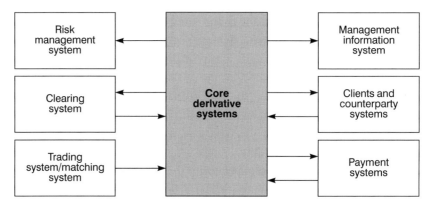

Figure 4.1 Generic links between systems

- What level and type of security policy is needed for the systems?
- What are the benefits and disadvantages of the systems used?
- What integration and interaction with other internal/external systems will occur?

Each of these questions must be answered if managers and supervisors are to be in control of the system's use in the operations area. How else can a benchmarking exercise be undertaken?

In measuring the system performance we first need to differentiate between the technical performance and the operational performance.

Technical performance

Policy on which system supplier, operating platform, etc. will normally be a decision that rests with a central IT function. Operations managers will naturally be involved in the deliberations. The IT area will decide whether the system is performing to the specifications required and will update, upgrade and maintain the systems or arrange for suppliers to do this. They also need to ensure back-up and disaster recovery/continuation contingencies.

Operational performance

This involves the Operations managers and supervisors monitoring the performance of the system in relation to the original objectives. Technical issues will come into this process such as system downtime and these will be logged and raised with the technical support team. Other performance issues will be the ability of the system to:

- Generate the data in the required format
- Produce timely data
- Handle products
- Complete functions such as margin and revaluation
- Interface with other systems

To be able to undertake this performance monitoring requirement, data will be required from:

- The system itself
- Users' evaluations

In both cases logs need to be maintained and received. This data must then be analysed to provide a continuous profile of the system from both technical and operational viewpoints. The analysis will concentrate on the impact of the system's performance on the workflow. The combination of the data and analysis of impact will permit the managers to monitor developments of new software and/or upgrading and replacement of systems. As changes, and in particular a switch to a new system, are not something that can be achieved immediately, the monitoring of system performance, and its impact, is vitally important. In terms of contingency planning, without a clear understanding of the system's role and the duration of each task in the process we cannot prioritize the processes in the event of any kind of system failure or problem. Security over data on systems is also a key issue. Logging on to the system needs to be monitored and verified as authorized. Password discipline must be enforced through education of its importance and effective controls.

Important questions for Operation managers are therefore what system performance monitoring by managers and supervisors should include, what is the source of the data and how it should be used.

The headline issues, as already noted, are reliability and capability. The data source about systems and performance needs to include relevant facts on the actual technical performance and the deliverable performance. The latter will be about how efficient the use of the system is by the Operations teams. The use of the data is crucial to planning and to dealing with expansion of business and products.

People and performance management

Turning now to people, it must be recognized that the performance of people is driven by their own motivation and that provided by their supervisors and managers. Measuring that performance is essential but is also potentially one of the most difficult tasks performed by the manager/supervisor. Traditional forms of performance measurement such as appraisals have merit provided they are done well. If they are not, the outcome is usually a major disaster. Most people believe they are doing well, some believe they are performing impressively. To be told otherwise is not easy to take even when the person concerned knows the facts to be true.

It is important to be aware that the supervisor and manager have very different roles in the team. Both are motivators and organizers (in different ways) and both sit in judgment on the individuals and the team. That judgment and the individual's expectations frequently conflict with each other and as a result relationships, performance (individual and the team) and working environment can change dramatically for the worse. How is this problem overcome?

The manager and supervisors must work out a policy towards staff that:

- Is motivating
- Is credible i.e. fair and consistent
- Is implemented
- Stands up to scrutiny
- Is within the HR policy in the organization
- Is within the law

Motivation

Motivation comes in various forms. There is financial inducement, career advancement through promotional promises, profit share, ranking or grade, travel and perks, etc. Real motivation is a mixture of recognition and reward. Reward does not have to be financial or even promotion. Reward means little at the end of the day if it is not justified. Reward must be fair and therefore the basis for reward must be flexible and not narrow. However, at the heart of it all is the recognition skill shown by managers and supervisors. This constitutes:

- Understanding of the processes and procedures being under-taken
- The role of individuals in these processes and procedures
- The measurement of performance
- The impact and influence of external relationships and counter-parts
- An understanding of the individual as a person
- Identifying, acknowledging and resolving problems
- Involving people in decisions and information
- Even-handed treatment and consistent policy towards issues and people
- Respecting people and their efforts

People usually need to have a respect for colleagues to be motivated and that is true at all levels. An example is a football team. If certain players are not performing and results go against the team, confidence is lost, respect for the coach begins to fade and the results get even worse.

Managers and supervisors earn respect because they demonstrate the ability to look and listen, to see problems and offer solutions, to take action and not sit on the fence, to be critical but fair. Respect for the managers leads to motivation.

Creating the motivational environment is important but there is danger. Consider the following potential situations:

■ Over-rewarding someone
■ Under-rewarding someone
■ Over-promoting
■ Under-promoting
■ Promising solutions that are not delivered
■ Over-criticizing
■ Under-reprimanding

For most managers these are the headline issues they will confront as they respond to different situations in the operation. Each of them presents the likelihood of an undermining of the manager's/ supervisor's respect in the ideas and minds of individuals and, usually, the team. Worse still, these views may not be obvious but the damage is nevertheless happening.

Many managers have been of the opinion that they manage their people superbly while the opposite view is taken by their staff. Sooner or later the problems will surface and by then it is too late. Managers and supervisors must take time to understand motivation, to reflect on the importance of issues to staff, even when the manager cannot see why it should be important.

Communication, listening and accepting that others may have ideas that are worthy of consideration, and being seen to take action and, above all, explain the reasons for the action are vital.

No motivation means trouble is brewing

The pitfalls that await the manager/supervisor are many. People are fickle, have great expectations far above what is achievable and can be given.

The risks associated with fairly routine manager/supervisor day-to-day work are highlighted in Table 4.1. However, underlying the principle of managing people is to assess how the individual performances are contributing to the overall performance of the team.

Performance measurement

Managers and supervisors will have a feel for how their team is performing and that feel is an essential benchmark. However, there needs to be more substance to the analysis of performance and this takes the form of comparisons, tracking and adjustments to procedures.

Analysis of workflow, through the use of workflow charts, for instance, will achieve two things:

- Provide the data needed to make any adjustment to structure and/ or procedures
- Show team members that management is aware of the current and potential future situations

Accurate management information on performance of individuals, the team, the procedures and the controls is vital for any realistic and

Table 4.1 Risks associated with routine work by managers and supervisors

Situation	Info/action/origin	Manager	Staff member/team	Risk
Salary review	Appraisal	Works within budget	Has expectations	High-risk potential of demotivation
New grade/recruitment	Appraisal/business growth/leavers	Works within head-count	Expect resolution but are concerned that new promotion/entrant does not affect their own prospects	High-risk potential of demotivation
Falling standards/performance	MI/feedback/complaints/growth in volumes/shortage of staff	Works within budget constraints	Expect resolution. Do not accept/understand business issues	Potential for dissatisfaction and negative reaction to any criticism
Personality clash	Feedback observation	HR considerations	Expect resolution. Probably two 'camps' supporting the individuals	Risk of appearing to support one or other protagonists. Demotivating for the 'losing' camp
Poor performer	Feedback appraisals	Must act	Team await the decision (may or may not have sympathy with individual)	Over- or under-reaction will both be badly received and demotivate

therefore meaningful assessments to be made. There is a danger that staff will interpret workflow analysis as having hidden agendas such as head-count reduction. Adequate involvement and communication will overcome this, particularly if the positive outcome of the process is explained.

Workflow analysis in generic terms provides data on:

- What is being processed and when
- How it is impacted by factors such as volume
- What resource is available
- Where pressure points are
- Where problems are or may occur
- What scope there is for change

By analysing the primary, secondary and periodic processes and tasks, their expected and actual duration and whether the resource is being optimized the managers can judge the performance level. They can also plan ahead, introduce change and have information to support their argument for change. These charts are simple to produce and maintain and provide credible support information essential to the day-to-day and long-term management of the Operations team.

Management of people

If we want to put this whole subject into perspective we need to draw together the issues outlined above and consider how these interact. We also need to consider any suitable external benchmarks. Figure 4.2 gives some ideas on this subject.

Figure 4.2 shows how sources of information are utilized to provide various viewpoints on the assessment of systems and people. This will enable managers to make informed decisions on everything from salaries and grades to system enhancement and procedure changes.

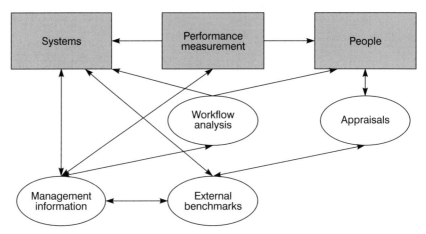

Figure 4.2 Using sources of information when assessing systems and people

In many cases the information is routinely available, in others it may need research, such as external benchmarks. Once it is obtained a whole range of options are available, all of which help in the managing people and system processes. A few examples would be:

■ Training requirements
■ System enhancements
■ Automation
■ Better working environment
■ Contingency planning
■ Business planning
■ Motivation

Benchmarking

One way of benchmarking that can be utilized is to use data produced by some clearing organizations that provide information on settlement performance, etc. Another source is to use external benchmarking organizations. One such company, GSCS Benchmarks, produces data about settlement, safekeeping and risk benchmarks.

EQUITIES HIGHLIGHTS

Total transactions per quarter – more than 3,030,000

Average settlement rate – 94.12%
Value of dividends collected – more than US$5.0 billion
Value of tax reclaims collected – more than US$80 million

SETTLEMENT	High	97.67	Japan	Low	62.08	Portugal
SAFEKEEPING		97.39	Japan		89.91	New Zealand
OPERATIONAL RISK		86.70	Germany		62.91	Portugal

FIXED INCOME HIGHLIGHTS

Total transactions per quarter – more than 306,000

Average settlement rate – 91.82%
Value of interest collected – more than US$3.3 billion
Value of tax reclaims collected – more than US$67 million

SETTLEMENT	High	98.43	Canada	Low	73.33	Netherlands
SAFEKEEPING		98.24	Japan		89.88	ICSDs
OPERATIONAL RISK		87.83	Canada		74.20	Netherlands

Figure 4.3 External benchmarking

As you can see from Figure 4.3, the Operations manager can utilize these benchmarks to identify the performance by country and product. It also allows the manager to assess the likelihood of problems in settlement or safekeeping in particular products and agents, as well as assessing risk.

There is a need to be wary of using a simple benchmark and there must also be an internal benchmark standard for tasks and processes. However, used in conjunction with, say, exchange benchmarks, a realistic view of how the operation is performing can be achieved.

Summary

Managing people and systems is not something to be taken lightly – the risk in doing so is too great. Communication and awareness are essential, respect must be earned and that can only be achieved with adequate information gleaned form sources such as appraisals, management information, workflow charts, etc. Underestimating the complexity of the task would be foolish as good managers are created, not born. Managing people and systems needs suitable management as well as technical skills, leadership and motivation to achieve the goal. The team needs these as well if it is to be moulded into a successful unit. Managers and supervisors must provide the drive for it to happen.

Chapter 5

Client services

The importance of client service

The concept of client service is as important in the settlement and support areas as it is in the front end of the business. Top-quality research, advisory and execution services are quite separate from the quality of the settlement services offered by the broker.

No longer does a client have to suffer inferior or costly services from either the front or back office of their broker. Prime brokerage, centralized and global derivative clearing have enabled clients to pick and choose, selecting several brokers for their skill and performance in various services and separating the chosen suppliers of execution and settlement. Of course, sometimes, as in the case of prime brokerage, it may be the same broker providing both, but Operations must recognize that clients can and will change their counterparty if the service is not good enough. It should be remembered that the in-house trading and dealing areas are as much clients as external counterparties.

We can see in Figure 5.1 that the client services team within operations is composed of two functions, client service (the day-to-day relationship) and relationship management. The relationship flow is obviously two-way and in addition the client services team will

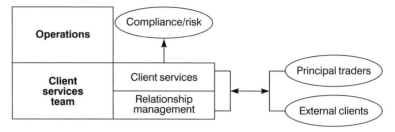

Figure 5.1 Relationship flow diagram

liaise with both compliance and risk management. This concept is explained as we explore the role in this chapter.

For Operations it is essential to recognize that clients are important, for the very existence of the Operations function is to service the trading and dealing. No clients, no Operations department, and the stark reality is that organizations are outsourcing Operations functions where the cost or performance of maintaining an in-house function makes little business sense. There are a number of benefits to the organization in outsourcing just as there are benefits in retaining a function in-house. However, if the in-house function is expensive, because of high error rates, etc., or is performing badly and losing clients, there is a powerful argument for dispensing with it. Of course, today we also have the cost of technology to consider and maintaining suitable systems infrastructure to support increasingly complex trading and settlement as well as more sophisticated client added-value services can also put a question mark against in-house Operations teams. The key to retaining an in-house Operations function is the ability to provide cost-effective and high-quality performance allied to an ability to sell some or all of the services to other parties. This is why we have firms that offer prime brokerage or derivatives clearing where they utilize the infrastructure needed to support the in-house trading and dealing by taking on all or some of the Operations functions of the client. Specialist firms are set up to in-source Operations functions (for instance, fund administration) and, of course, custodians are continuously expanding the range of services they offer clients.

We can see that there is significant competition in the field of Operations and as rationalization of the industry continues so that competition intensifies. The assumption must be that Operations is now very much a product and as such it can be bought and sold. With regulatory and risk issues, including operational risk capital, being set alongside running and development costs, an Operations function needs to be run as a business, as we saw in Chapter 2.

Business culture

This requires two cultures to be developed within the Operations teams. First, we need a business culture and it is important to put personnel through a continuous business awareness training programme to achieve this. These programmes must be tailored for the business concerned and will typically cover:

- Business profile and objectives
- The 'market' and the competition
- Cost of money
- Budgets
- Efficiency and the impact of errors and poor performance
- Understanding the client's business
- Developing services
- How the image of the company must be created and maintained in the marketplace
- Operating standards must be kept high
- Good skill sets are needed and must be developed
- Client retention is a crucial objective
- Awareness of the competition is paramount
- Planning is crucial in a rapidly changing industry

The implementation of this type of programme has to happen as it is highly unlikely that technical skills alone will ensure the kind of performance and standard of service delivery by themselves. Developing an understanding of finance so that control of costs and profitability can become part of the team's thinking is just as important as instilling the understanding of importance of reputation and consistency of performance.

Client culture

The second culture is the client service culture. This can have various definitions and will be different in, say, fund manager or retail markets from that within a broker or bank and varies in some respects depending on the client. Part of the client culture comes from business awareness in the fact that understanding the client's business is vital if we are to design a service that meets their requirement, and, just as importantly, enables us to develop added-value services as bespoke solutions for the client. The latter, of course, will have the effect of setting our product apart from the competition.

There is a tendency to assume that client service is a relatively straightforward subject and that most people are naturally going to recognize the need to be polite to a customer etc. To some extent that is true but equally hearing the same 'customer announcement' each morning apologizing for the delay to your train and for the inconvenience caused does not constitute good client service. It is certainly polite but it does not provide a solution to the problem. In fact in the end such announcements can create a massive negative reaction by the customer because they do not believe them to be sincere or of any useful purpose.

It is also vitally important to remember that although a client may not seem important because they are not trading a large volume or deal only once in a while, they may be as important to a firm as to an organization. For instance, Operations teams may not be aware of that type of client's involvement in the corporate finance services the firm offers and which earn high fees. It must be instilled in the team that all clients must receive a high standard of service regardless of size or earnings.

For most organizations client service is two-way with relationships with both external clients and external suppliers, where in order to provide a good level of service to our clients, the service that is received from other parties must be of a high standard. This has a direct bearing on the level of service that can be provided to clients and managing that kind of relationship, as we saw in the previous chapter, is very important.

The role of the client services team

Arguably the most important role that the team has is to understand the client and what is important to the client. Most brokers can provide services on a wide range of markets and products. Most offer some kind of system and data access and other technology-related services. Almost all are prepared to accommodate single-currency settlement and accept a wide variety of collateral. In short there are many 'standard' client services available.

What sets one broker apart from its competitors is the ability of its client team to recognize issues that will, or potentially will, affect the client. Into this category falls:

- Trading new products or markets
- Collateral management
- Technology-related services
- Regulatory issues
- Accounting and taxation issues
- Domestic and global industry developments
- Marketing
- Clients of the client
- Pricing business and high-level relationship management

However, there is also the simple but critically important aspect of providing timely and correct responses to problems and queries.

It must be remembered that in many cases the client does not have massive operational resource to deal with the complex business it undertakes and therefore relies largely on the support provided by its broker or brokers. Nor does it have the day-to-day exposure to the industry which brokers' staff experience. Issues that are routine to the broker's Operations staff may not be understood or their importance recognized by the client's Operations staff. It is easy for a broker to assume that a deadline or process or procedure is recognized and understood by the client, only to find that a problem is created. Hand-holding, particularly for new entrants to a market such as the derivatives part of the industry and operational support, are crucial to enabling that client to undertake business. In providing solutions for the client the relationship strengthens and grows as the client feels confident in expanding its business. Thus Operations has contributed to the firm gaining additional business and revenue.

However, the team needs to be skilled not only in understanding the kind of issues that may cause a problem but also in recognizing when those issues will create a problem. The ability to pre-empt a problem is of real benefit to the client and will be appreciated.

The client services role therefore is partly managing the settlement of the client's business and partly managing and developing a relationship with the client. It is not easy and while the 'client service' team may front this they rely on every part of the Operations function performing to ensure that the service delivered is of the required standard.

Resource management

In many organizations, the client service team is seen as having the 'best' job in the Operations area. This is because they often visit clients either locally or overseas and can also be required to entertain them with lunches or corporate events. I would venture to suggest that it may be 'a touch of the grass is greener' because no amount of corporate entertaining or jetting around the world compensates for having to listen to a client complaining about poor treatment or, worse, telling you they are transferring their business to a competitor. Some clients are, of course, very difficult to deal with and can be aggressive, demanding and in some cases quite unreasonable in their demands. Happily most clients are usually fairly easy to work with. Some require a significant level of support while others can require only the core service.

Some problems that occur are outside the scope of the client services team. Internal politics at the client, for instance, can happen and there is no way that the client services team can or should get involved in this, although, of course, they will need to manage the impact and implications of such a problem.

It is the client service team which is the face of the firm for the outside world and therefore their role is extremely important. They are often the first contact and sometimes the only contact that clients have with the firm, so the image that they portray and represent is crucial.

All of this, however, does not get away from the fact that the manager can be faced with some parts of the Operations team viewing the client services team as elite, and indeed the client services team may think this themselves. In reality, as noted above, this should not be the case as client service is about teamwork, and it must be carefully managed to ensure that everyone feels part of it and that the whole Operations team is working towards the same goal and understand the importance of looking after the client. If this is not the case then eventually the service to clients will suffer, which will lead to less business, which then affects everybody.

In order to provide quality client service then a specialized, dedicated team of people needs to be developed to focus on the issues and enforce the disciplines that are needed. Personnel in the client services function need specialist skills and the right personality in order to be able to perform their function. These mostly include:

- *Excellent communication skills* – the need to be able to communicate effectively and clearly with people at different levels both within and outside the organization. This involves efficient dissemination of information.
- *Excellent working knowledge of the products* – it is essential that personnel have a broad knowledge of the markets and products that clients use. It also requires them to know where to find reliable information to be able to provide clients with a speedy response to questions.
- *Confidence* – personnel must build up the trust of clients and to do this they must appear confident in the advice and responses that they give to clients. They must be confident in their abilities but must never appear over-confident and make the client feel incompetent.
- *Patience and politeness* – sometimes clients will test the patience of personnel. This may be frustration, or a lack of understanding of the matter in hand, or due to problems that are perceived, rightly or wrongly, to have been caused by the firm. Defusing the situation and explaining the way in which the matter can be resolved takes great skill (see next point).
- *Tact and diplomacy* – personnel must be able to display tact when dealing with difficult situations. This includes when the client may believe that they are right even when they are not. There are always going to be difficult clients to deal with who need careful handling. Sometimes personnel will need diplomatic skills to cope with situations such as where the client is not performing settlement correctly or there is a risk management issue. When meeting clients, personnel must know the limits of information about the firm and about solutions for other clients that can be shared.
- *Social skills* – When meeting clients, personnel need to have confidence to be able to converse with clients at various levels of

seniority. When representing the company they must conduct themselves in an appropriate manner.

- *Teamwork skills* – it is essential that personnel have team skills and people management skills and are able to work effectively with groups of people.
- *Business skills* – personnel must be encouraged not only to look at the specific job or function that they are performing but must also think about the business as a whole. This involves vision and allows them to provide input to the running of other areas drawing on the experience that they have from their own area. This is relevant across all Operations areas and is not specific to client services, but must be managed as a constructive process.
- *Presentation and marketing skills* – from time to time personnel may be called upon to make presentations to the client about various aspects of the services provided, settlement processes, new products or procedures. Clients need to be kept up to date with developments in the markets and personnel will need skills to be able to present information to clients and to be able to clearly explain certain procedures. At all times client service personnel are presenting the firm to the client and should keep this in mind by being aware of opportunities to promote the company.

The manager's task is to build and resource an Operations team with the right people and skills and to then build additional skills and resource into a client services team. There are various ways to achieve this.

Client services and relationship management

In an organization, client services might be split into two parts: client services and relationship management. The possible role of each is shown in the following:

Client services	Relationship management
Daily operations contact	Service proposals
Account maintenance	Client presentations
Settlements	Pricing of new and existing business
Risk management	Measurement and monitoring of relationships
Margining compliance	Developing existing relationships
Documentation	Client technology, system training/support
Systems organization	Marketing of services to new clients
Added-value services	Development of client database
	Responsibility for corporate entertainment
	Effective communication within the organization
	Customer Coordination Group

Client services

This team would be responsible for the day-to-day running of the clients' accounts. This involves routine settlement, agreement of fund and collateral movements, maintenance of static data on client accounts and that documentation is all in place.

Client services has a key role to play in risk management, as they are familiar with the client and the processes for settlement. They should be sensitive to any changes in the clients' settlement procedures and would be aware of any likely problems that may occur. This may include sudden changes of payment details, untimely settlement and unusual trading patterns or products. This data needs to be communicated to the risk management function.

Client services are the first point of contact for any problems the client might experience with the output or performance in the case of direct access of the systems run by the firm. They need to be able to help to solve some of the fundamental problems that could occur such as errors, difficulties with access, etc. In addition, they need to liaise with the IT team to ensure that the client's problem is dealt with promptly and efficiently and that the same problems are not being encountered repeatedly. As the client services team have the day-to-day contact with the clients then they should be involved in the development of the systems used. They have useful input because they know what is important to clients and what would help to make the settlement process more efficient from both the clients' and the firm's perspectives.

Relationship management

This team would be responsible for looking after the client's accounts at a relationship level rather than at a day-to-day operational level although, of course, there will be a high degree of interaction with the client services function. The role involves marketing and making presentations to new clients as well as developing existing relationships. In order to ensure that client business is profitable, the relationship management team is responsible for analysing the revenue derived from each major client.

It is essential that the relationship management team have a role in developing existing relationships as well as attracting new ones. It is easy to become complacent with existing client relationships and expect loyalty to continue unabated. This is a very short-sighted view given that we have noted how competitive the marketplace is and that there will always be another organization who is trying to tempt the clients away and gain their business. Even though the client in question may not be very active, there must be a discipline within the relationship management team to contact clients on a regular basis, just to say 'hello' and let them know that you care. This might seem a little unnecessary but it is the contacts that continue when there is no immediate gain in terms of revenue that are more often than not turned to when the revenue-generating business is there. Put another way, today's small client is potentially tomorrow's major client.

Experience often shows that you can learn a lot from such calls to 'quiet' accounts. For example, it may be that one of the client's head dealers has left and it has taken a long time to recruit a replacement but a new dealer is due to start very soon and therefore activity is expected to increase dramatically within a short period of time. Obviously this example is a case of being in the right place at the right time but imagine how pleased the client was to get the call. It may be the difference between them continuing their business with your firm, as opposed to letting the new dealer decide where the business should go. This also demonstrates that there can be significant importance in the back office-to-back office relationship and the trust that exists.

Possession of information and responding accordingly is a fundamental part of client relationship management. It is therefore important that data be maintained about the client, contacts with the client including mailings, logs about problems and other contacts such as routine meetings. Figure 5.2 shows a generic information flow.

The client report is crucial and procedures need to be in place to ensure that these are completed. In some cases client meetings will be joint front office/Operations and sometimes the salesperson or Operations will meet with the client separately. Client meeting reports should be held centrally and be available to both sales teams and client services personnel. However, sensitive information that is not for general sight needs to be recorded and held separately.

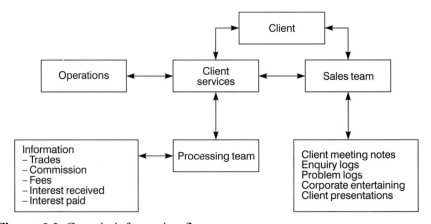

Figure 5.2 Generic information flow

Obviously the two parts of the client services team in Operations must work together and share information about the clients' activities but it is even more imperative that the whole Operations team works together and also in conjunction with the sales desk in order to provide the best possible service to clients.

Maintaining the quality approach and dealing with difficult clients

It is also important to deliver the support and services in the right and appropriate manner. Often today the services offered will be subject to legal documentation in the form of service level agreements or something similar. This is crucial for packages like prime brokerage, custody, fund administration or outsourced operations as the terms under which the service is supplied are the guidelines for resolving any significant problems as well as protecting both parties against operational risk.

Clearly a firm cannot always provide a solution or pre-empt a problem. When an issue arises it must be dealt with in a sympathetic but firm way. Some problems are the results of mistakes and misunderstanding, and can originate from both parties. These will be resolved in the process of managing the relationship.

However, it must also be recognized that certain problems are not just mistakes. They are serious issues that could put the firm or the client at risk. There could be situations of fraud or money laundering or they may be just an attempt to manipulate the system to gain an advantage.

Case study 1

For instance, if a client has a margin call today for, say, £100 000 for a position opened yesterday and the collateral is not received today, what could be the reasons?

The answer is there are many possible reasons. Of these most will be perfectly understandable but it is possible that the client is taking the position for a very short time, say two days, and has no intention of providing the collateral. The client service team must be able to assess the situation correctly and act accordingly.

Whatever the situation the broker must always act in accordance with the rules and regulations applicable to it *even if by doing that the client threatens to move its business*.

Of course, no one likes to lose a client, least of all one that pays a high level of commission. Sometimes the 'difficult' client may simply be embarrassed at their lack of understanding or may be suffering severe internal problems with resource, experience, systems, dealers, etc. Clients who expect brokers to bend or break the rules to accommodate them are clients not worth having, as they could, and ultimately will, put the whole business at risk. Clients worth having are those who listen to reasons why certain requests cannot be accommodated, and understand that it is not the firm being difficult but acting in accordance with proper business practice and, more importantly, the regulatory requirement. Consider the following case study concerning money laundering.

Case study 2

The following typology is provided as an example of how funds could be laundered using the derivatives market.

In this method, the broker must be willing to allocate genuinely losing trades to the account in which criminal proceeds are deposited. Instead of relying on misleading or false documentation, the broker uses the genuine loss-making documentation to be allocated to the detriment of the dirty money account holder. As an example, a broker uses two accounts, one called 'A' into which the client regularly deposits money that needs laundering, and one called 'B' which is intended to receive the laundered funds. The broker enters the trading market and 'goes long' (purchases) 100 derivative contracts of a commodity, trading at an offer price of $85.02, with a 'tick' size of $25. At the same time he 'goes short' (sells) 100 contracts of the same commodity at the bid price of $85.00. At that moment, he has two legitimate contracts which have been cleared through the floor of the exchange.

Later in the trading day, the contract price has altered to $84.72 bid and $84.74 offered. The broker returns to the market, closing both open positions at the prevailing prices. Now, the broker, in his own books, assigns the original purchase at $85.02 and the subsequent sale at $84.72 to account A. The percentage difference between the two prices is 30 points or ticks (the difference between $84.72 and $85.02). To calculate the loss on this contract, the tick size which is $25 is multiplied by the number of contracts, 100, multiplied by the price movement, 30. Thus: $25 \times 100 \times 30 = \$75\,000$ (loss).

The other trades are allocated to the B account, which following the same calculation theory of tick size multiplied by the number of contracts multiplied by the price movement results in a profit as follows: $25 \times 100 \times 26 = \$65\,000$ (profit). The account containing the money to be laundered has just paid out $75 000 for the privilege of receiving a profit of $65 000 on the other side. In other words, the launderer has paid $10 000 for the privilege of successfully laundering $75 000. Such a sum is well within the amount of premium which professional launderers are prepared to pay for the privilege of cleaning up such money. As a transaction, it is perfectly lawful from the point of view of the broker. He has not taken the risk of creating false documentation, which could conceivably be discovered, and everything has been done in full sight of the market.

Source: The Joint Money Laundering Steering Committee, *Guidance Notes for the Financial Sector*, December 2001 edition

Managers need to make the teams aware of what can and cannot be tolerated in a relationship. Adequate procedures are a must and these need to be fully documented, approved by compliance and the risk managers and enforced, even in the face of pressure from sales or traders.

The power of close-out is crucial as obligations may have been assumed by the firm on behalf of the client and therefore these pose a significant risk. There is a massive difference between a genuine error or a problem for a day or two and a serious, potentially catastrophic situation.

Escalation of situations must also be an automatic process so that there is no risk of someone agreeing to a situation who is neither experienced enough to make the decision or empowered to do so.

Procedures and controls

The client services function, if it is doing its job, will make every effort to identify the problems and then address the issue within the established procedures and controls framework. To be done effectively this can only be achieved by building the relationship at every level. This is particularly at day-to-day operational level where most problems and issues will originate. The team needs therefore to possess a high level of communication skills at all levels to enable it to deal with sensitive issues and to get to the root of any problems. These skills are also needed to communicate internally with the relevant parties, i.e. front office, compliance, risk, etc.

Part of the controls will be procedures that log the activity of the client as well as documenting any problems generated by either party, the cause and time it took to resolve and the outcome including any financial loss, regulatory action, etc.

Service quality and delivery

Providing a quality service neither entails jumping every time the client shouts nor agreeing to anything the client does or wants. It does, however, entail a considered approach, an understanding of the issues, firm and correct action and a high level of communication. A mutual respect of each other's roles and functions will form a good base for client relationships but, most importantly, the service standard agreed should be deliverable.

There is no point at all in overselling the services and then delivering a poor performance. There are many performance measurements that occur in the financial services industry (for instance, fund managers' performance is continuously measured against standard benchmarks). This benchmarking of services also applies to Operations-based functions such as custody and effectively any client acting professionally and in accordance with best practice and regulation will measure performance.

It is better to set out exactly what can and cannot be delivered, agree the standard for the service, agree to develop other required services (if appropriate) and begin a long successful relationship than to lie to gain the client and lose them in acrimonious circumstances a few months later.

Reputation is everything and surprisingly, given the size of the industry, word spreads quickly and a situation such as the one above could cause irreparable damage.

Managing added-value services

In a bid to be different from the competition, many brokers try to identify and develop 'added-value services' for clients. Examples of added-value services that are typically offered by brokers are:

- Client technology systems and data access
- Internet sites
- Message facilities
- Provision of information such as global product details, publications, trading calendars and market news and updates
- Tailored client reporting
- Regulatory reporting
- Training

Two issues are important here; is the service really needed and is it cost effective?

Very often well-intentioned ideas, which are expected to gain and retain clients, actually prove to be expensive and have little success. This can be because:

- The product has been developed by the broker and therefore reflects the broker's perception of what is needed and is not much use to the clients
- It has been requested by the client but the likely actual usage has not been ascertained
- It has a significant impact on the broker's operations area
- It requires unplanned and unbudgeted system development and on-going maintenance
- It incurs costs that cannot be reclaimed via higher commission charges

Good added-value services can be a winner but careful management of what is offered, how it is offered and to whom it is offered is critically important. In most organizations certain special requests from clients are met but must be carefully controlled and only granted under certain circumstances or a major and costly commitment may be the result as the following case study shows.

Case study 3

We can look at custodians and system suppliers to illustrate the type of problem. For the custodians and service suppliers such as system companies there is a core service that is offered.

Custodians then develop added-value services but even these tend to be standard offering in most cases. Although not specifically developed in bespoke fashion for each customer this can prove costly and needs a high take-up by the customers to be worth while, but of course custodians are in competition with each other as well as other organizations such as the central securities depositories and need to make their product as comprehensive and attractive as possible to the client.

System suppliers face a similar decision: do they meet client requests for additional capabilities over and above the core products? With the systems it is quite probable that each client has a bespoke requirement. This may not be particularly different from the main product and in some cases a simple solution is possible. However, once a system supplier starts developing and supporting a range of bespoke products they can find themselves in an escalating commitment that may produce very little in the way of additional revenue, uses up valuable resource and may well end up being provided at a loss. They cannot even resell the bespoke product in most cases because, of course, the client wants it to gain an advantage over their

> competitors. Today the system suppliers are far less likely to develop bespoke products and instead concentrate on the number-crunching and core products leaving the clients to use packages internally to bespoke the product.

With added-value, bespoke and exclusive services there is a real need for effective management. Each client's request must be judged on a case-by-case basis and the decision must be made according to a cost–benefit analysis produced by the relationship management team and the business managers. Part of the process will also involve risk management to determine whether there is any positive or negative risk implications and compliance to ensure that no regulatory problems will occur. Finally, if the bespoke development is given the go-ahead, the legal department needs to ensure that the agreements are updated, amended or adapted to remove any exposure to legal claims.

Added-value services are strong selling points but, as we can see, they are also potential time bombs.

Successful interaction with other internal areas

In today's markets there is so much multiple product trading that there will be, at various times, interaction between various departments and different areas of an organization, and often with parties externally and overseas. The impact of global trading on these different areas varies but it is very important to recognize when and where the impact will occur and how this affects the firm's ability to ultimately deliver a quality service to its internal and external clients.

Good interaction across an organization and with its external agents and counterparties creates a better all-round service to the client as well as reducing costs and benefiting risk management. To achieve this managers need to create business awareness, risk and client cultures not just in a client service team but across the whole Operations function. Understanding the big picture is a cliché that is in fact very pertinent.

Building client relationships and loyalty

It is often assumed that client entertaining is essential to relationship building and keeping a client loyal. Cynics say it is bribery and quite rightly regulators want to make sure that there is no abuse or detrimental impact for the clients of the client.

Used in the right way a client is likely to appreciate it as a thank-you and an opportunity to develop the relationship and discuss critical issues, but it also has important implications for the client service teams. In most cases copious amounts of client entertaining is not necessary, or wanted; the important thing for most clients is the quality of the service. Therefore the use of client entertaining to compensate for the problem of poor service is not satisfactory and almost certainly will not have the desired impact.

However, client entertaining can enable discussion to take place about issues that cannot or should not be the subject of phone calls or formal meetings. This applies at all levels and a considerable amount of practical and profitable discussion can take place if the event is planned properly.

We have already mentioned several times that servicing clients is about a team effort from Operations and not just about the client service team. Therefore, it is a good idea for managers to involve members of the Operations team when meeting and entertaining clients. This allows people who work in the trade processing areas, for example, to meet clients, understand their business and comprehend the impact that they individually can have on the service provided to the client and ultimately on the client's business.

This can work in two ways as benefits can be gained from the client by also involving their staff who would otherwise never be included in meetings and corporate entertainment. It is always advantageous to have as many different contacts within the client's organization as possible. In that way you will get to know the client and their business better. Also there is not so much of a risk of the relationship deteriorating if the main contact was to leave the employment of the client, or the main contact at the firm was to leave and go to a competing firm.

It is important to have a good record of how often a client receives any form of entertaining. It is also essential to get the attendees from the team to complete a post-event client report, just as they would for a normal client meeting, within a day or two at most. This report should contain actual and perceived issues and suggested or confirmed follow-up actions. Client entertaining should be both enjoyable and productive for both client and broker.

To summarize client service, we can say that the Operations manager needs to be aware of:

- The importance of managing the service provided to the client to agreed standards
- The need to review the changes in the market and to respond with new or upgraded services
- The implications for operational risk of providing various services
- The need to make sure that client service teams understand their responsibilities to support the client but to do so within the controls and risk requirements of the firm
- The importance of regulatory issues such as client money, money laundering and fraud
- The requirement to develop processes, procedures and controls for the client service product
- The need to ensure communication and interaction with other Operations and business areas is good and works to the benefit of the organization as a whole.

Chapter 6

The relationship with regulation

A firm must deal with its regulators in an open and co-operative

way, and must disclose to the FSA appropriately anything relating

to the firm of which the FSA would reasonably expect notice.

(Principle 11, The Financial Services Authority (UK) Handbook)

It may seem a little obvious but Operations functions have regulation to comply with and that regulation comes from several different sources. Complying with this regulation is a key part of the role of Operations and so the manager and team need to be aware of their responsibilities in achieving this. As the level of regulation varies and some regulation can be very specific to a part of the function or even a process within the function, there is a risk that a failure to recognize or comply with a regulation could occur. This is very much the case for an organization with a diverse business or one that is heavily involved in international business and therefore operates under different regulators and regulation.

Regulation that applies to Operations is often complex, dealing as it does with everything from client protection to reporting requirements. Both the regulator in the jurisdiction and various other organizations that have rules such as exchanges and clearing houses set out the regulation. Compliance departments will play a major role in ensuring that these regulations are complied with and so we need to consider the relationship with compliance as well as that with the regulators. It is the case with most regulators that copious amounts of information about the regulatory environment is readily available and a process of consultation and briefings is carried out before regulation is changed or new regulation introduced. We saw in one of the previous chapters how it is important for Operations managers to be prepared to be involved in industry committees, etc. and it is therefore also important that, in conjunction with the compliance officer, the Operations manager is being made aware of and is providing input to proposed changes.

The relationship with regulation should be viewed as a positive rather than negative situation: regulation, after all, is designed to protect and reduce risk. It may well be that the actual regulatory requirements are detailed and occupy time and resource in meeting them and yet everyone should understand that without regulation there would be a much smaller industry.

The relationship with regulators, given the complexity of regulation over the whole business and high-level non-operations issues, is, as we have already noted, managed by compliance. The Operations relationship is by and large one of running procedures and processes within the regulatory guideline, reporting relevant data to regulatory bodies and implementing controls that will ensure compliance with the rules and regulations.

Some aspects of this are also a matter of law such as money laundering and in the UK there is requirement to report any suspicious situation to the appointed Money Laundering Reporting Officer (MLRO). Compliance and Operations managers must ensure that staff are both aware of the money-laundering rules and know who their MLRO is. They must also ensure that staff understand how a money-laundering situation might arise. Some types of investment activity lend themselves to money laundering, for instance derivatives where there is potentially a daily cash settlement process and also cash collateral. Staff must be aware of the client relationship and also the regulatory relationship. This is not easy as the client is a source of revenue and the staff member has been trained to treat the client accordingly and yet they are also being told that anything suspicious must be reported. The problem is that a perfectly reasonable request from an Operations point of view may actually be a money-laundering situation. Consider again the extract from the Joint Money Laundering Steering Group, *Guidance Notes for the Financial Sector* in Case study 2.

For many Operations managers the whole concept of managing regulatory requirements within the framework of the operations processing function is a significant challenge and yet the relationship with regulation is there all the time and must be dealt with. The following comment, again from the Joint Money Laundering Steering Group, sums up the situation in the UK in the aftermath of the change to the regulatory structure (N2) that took place in 2001:

> *Running a business in the post N2 era can be a minefield. New or revised regulations, procedures and practices are being introduced frequently, resulting in operational and strategic challenges for senior management. Every successful organisation within the financial services arena constantly balances profitability with compliance . . .*

The regulators in a jurisdiction are not solely concerned with rules and regulations over trading, clearing, settlement and custody. Frequently they are also concerned with standards, ethics and competence.

One significant relationship with the regulator that Operations may have is in the area of competence and qualified personnel. Training and examinations to establish competency have long been required in the front-office environment and are increasingly being introduced in the Operations areas. Ultimately licences to carry out operational functions will be granted and revoked on the basis of the competency of the people in the team. In Chapter 3 we saw how Clearnet have requirements for systems and resource standards that if not met can lead to suspension or revoking of membership.

As regulators seek to introduce higher standards and qualifications for Operations-based staff it is important that the Operations manager can train and/or recruit suitably qualified people and that systems, infrastructure and processes are meeting the regulatory standards laid down.

Many regulatory requirements are related to other relationships, primarily clients. In the UK the FSA Principles reflect this. The eleven principles are:

1 Integrity
   A *firm* must conduct its business integrity
2 Skill, care and diligence
   A *firm* must conduct its business with due skill, care and diligence
3 Management and control
   A *firm* must take reasonable care to organise and control its affairs responsibly and effectively, with adequate risk management systems
4 Financial prudence
   A *firm* must maintain adequate financial resources
5 Market conduct
   A *firm* must observe proper standards of market conduct
6 Customers' interests
   A *firm* must pay due regard to the interest of its *customers* and treat them fairly
7 Communications with clients
   A *firm* must pay due regard to the information needs of its *clients*, and communicate information to them in a way which is clear, fair and not misleading
8 Conflicts of interest
   A *firm* must manage conflicts of interest fairly, both between itself and its *customers* and between itself and its *customers* and between a *customer* and another *client*

9 Customers: relationships of trust

A *firm* must take reasonable care to ensure the suitability of its advice and discretionary decisions for any *customer* who is entitled to rely upon its judgement

10 Clients' assets

A *firm* must arrange adequate protection for *clients'* assets when it is responsible for them

11 Relations with regulators

A *firm* must deal with its regulators in an open and cooperative way, and must disclose to the *FSA* appropriately anything relating to the *firm* of which the *FSA* would reasonably expect notice

(*Source*: FSA Handbook Release 001, December 2001)

The FSA states that 'The Principles are a general statement of the fundamental obligations of firms under the regulatory system'.

It is no surprise then that a failure to adhere to the Principles results in severe action against the firm that is in breach of them. However, Principle 11 with which we started this chapter also shows that the FSA is determined that the regulation is best enforced through cooperation, by receiving information from the firms and 'being close' to the firm. As they say, this is a less obtrusive way of monitoring its member firms.

Operations functions have direct and indirect processes that relate to many of the Principles and so could be in breach of them at times. Clearly errors and problems will occur and when they do it is imperative that the Regulator is informed if they might have caused a breach of the rules. If they are not notified or, worse, still not even recognized as being breaches and are subsequently discovered in a regulatory audit the outcome will be dire for the firm.

An Operations relationship with regulation, be it through compliance or direct as a member of an organization, is an important one. International and national regulators are constantly changing regulation to meet the changes in the industry and it is an ongoing task to remain fully aware of the relevant rules and Principles.

Different organizations have different regulators, rules and regulations to deal with. Within that regulation will be exemptions, authorizations and reporting requirements. In addition to the national regulators there are European Directives, Trustee requirements and exchange/clearing house regulations. There is also the law that applies to business and for which there are criminal offences and documentation that is needed as evidence that rules and regulations are complied with and to protect both client and firm.

Contrary to some people's views, regulation is not the hindrance to business, it is the firms that consistently breach regulations and put clients assets, not to mention other firms, at risk that is why regulation is needed.

Each regulatory jurisdiction will have competency standards and these need incorporating into a suitable development programme. As a very minimum to effectively manage the regulatory environment the operations manager must deal with the following issues:

- Regulatory awareness
- Competency
- Qualifications

Regulatory awareness

This encompasses two areas: internal and external rules and regulations. Training to regulatory qualification standard needs to be supplemented by in-house training on systems and procedures relevant to regulatory requirements and internal controls.

Competency

Continuous monitoring of individual and team awareness and capability must be undertaken together with any relevant benchmark such as industry-approved courses and training. It should form part of the appraisal process and be linked to the individual's current and future work and the business profile of the firm.

We can illustrate how a regulator approaches this by looking at the following extract from a speech by Hugh Davies, Chairman, Financial Services Authority on Training and Competence, 2 November 2000, entitled 'The need for greater professionalism amongst finance sector staff'.

... Financial services may not be the oldest profession but it does have a long history and ideas of what is and is not professional behaviour have developed. Standard [dictionary] definitions mention competence and skill and encapsulate ideas of:

- efficiency and effectiveness implying a standard against which performance is being assessed,
- acting with integrity,
- achieving to the best of your ability *or* taking pride in your work,
- commitment to training and development to deliver excellent results.

As Regulator we are interested in all these. They are crucial to the achievement of our statutory objectives. And integrity is the central component of our principles for businesses, and our principles for individuals.

Competence

A key element of professionalism is competence. Competence is important because it underpins performance – the performance of everyone from senior management to junior members of staff.

Ensuring satisfactory levels of competence is a prerequisite for achieving all of the FSA's statutory objectives – consumer protection, market confidence, public awareness and the reduction of financial crime. Standards of competence, more broadly, are also key to the successful development of the UK's international position. The availability of suitably trained and competent staff is almost always cited as the most important factor determining business location in this industry. So if we can, together, enhance the industry's professionalism, we can contribute positively to promoting one of the UK's key competitive advantages. Training is not an optional on-cost. It is the foundation stone of a successful strategy.

Training and Competence

In developing a new framework of rules on Training and Competence we inherited a wide variety of existing regimes.

Some industry sectors have been used to a detailed, prescriptive approach while for others Training and Competence was less explicit within their supervisory framework, though may have been linked to other supervisory principles such as the fit and proper criteria. We also were acutely aware that the attention paid to Training and Competence varied as a result.

In future, we shall want to recognize the efforts of firms that understood the importance of competence and its direct contribution to improving profitability through better performance. We aim to encourage firms which already have well developed policies and procedures in place by allowing sufficient freedom to continue to build on best practice. There's no point in our imposing our own set ideas on companies already doing well. Yet at the same time we also need to establish a regime which will ensure a consistent acceptable minimum level of competence. That is the tension we face.

In setting out what we require, the challenge has been to find a coherent framework and a form of words that will work with many different types of organization, from banks, through insurers to brokers, fund managers and IFAs. Now, for the first time, there will be a single, unified framework, which applies to all firms, in a clear and consistent way.

The message is that both regulation and training entered into willingly will be more effective, robust and likely to raise standards beyond minimum levels.

This also makes good business sense. How firms choose to do this is for them to decide but investing the time and effort to get it right before things go wrong must surely be better than sorting out problems after they happen. As part of that process we want to help firms to see why just settling for the minimum is a poor business decision.

Firms where a 'more than mechanical compliance' culture permeates the business and is evident in the way staff carry out their day-to-day work. You could argue that where a firm does not assess the competence of its staff, or has difficulty thinking through its training strategy, it will also have trouble thinking through other aspects of compliance. Training and Competence is, if you like, a litmus test of a firm's overall compliance culture.

Administration Functions

The scope of the FSA's Training and Competence régime, in terms of the people covered, largely mirrors the coverage of the current regulators. But, in line with our drive for a consistent approach across the whole industry, we will be extending the requirements for standards from the investment management sector to administration functions in life and pension back offices. This proposal, which applies to the supervisors or team leaders in back offices, was subject to a cost–benefit analysis. Many respondents were strongly in favour of this extension, giving improved customer service standards as the main reason for their support. Other benefits mentioned included:

- 'it will assist staff commitment and loyalty'
- 'many errors are due to lack of knowledge amongst processing staff'
- 'back office staff should be properly qualified'.

Some respondents emphasised benefits such as the likelihood of an improved compliance culture in firms and the better opportunities for staff that training provided.

In the consultation process suggestions were also made that we bring into the fold those involved in execution only business, compliance officers, marketing staff and a number of other groups. We will consider these suggestions but do not intend to widen the scope further at the start, save for any Training and Competence implications which emerge from our work on stakeholder pensions.

Qualifications

Managers must identify relevant qualifications for different team members. This will include, where appropriate and practical, recognized qualifications in the UK and Europe, the USA and Japan plus any jurisdiction where a reasonable and constant level of business is undertaken. Qualifications should be linked to the basic competency requirements of the regulators, exchanges and clearing houses as well as the business profile of the firm.

A programme to achieve the above objectives should be devised in conjunction with the compliance and human resources areas and should be an ongoing part of the resource management programme. The levels of training and qualifications should be reviewed and updated at least every six months and new staff should be required to complete a suitable industry-recognized training programme plus a series of suitable in-house or public non-examination product-awareness courses within two years of joining.

The manager must also ensure that all staff feel comfortable with their responsibilities and know how to escalate an issue that may be or may become a regulatory problem.

We started off the chapter with FSA Principle 11 and it is worth closing with the same statement as it encapsulates the whole relationship situation:

> *A firm must deal with its regulators in an open and co-operative*
>
> *way, and must disclose to the FSA appropriately anything relating*
>
> *to the firm of which the FSA would reasonably expect notice.*
>
> *(Principle 11, The Financial Services Authority (UK) Handbook)*

Chapter 7

Compliance and audit

In the previous chapter we considered the relationship that Operations teams have with regulators. Part of that relationship is managed through compliance and also the audit function. The relationship with both compliance and audit needs to be good so that the overall risk control and regulatory compliance is strong. Compliance and audit both have specific roles to play and so the way in which Operations interacts with each of them is important.

To some degree and in most organizations both compliance and audit are looked on with a mix of suspicion and fear. Neither, of course, is valid unless either the individual or team knows that they are not following procedures or are undertaking illegal activity. To understand the relationship issues we need to look at the roles of compliance and audit.

Compliance

A compliance function has two principal areas of responsibility:

- To create, implement and maintain suitable internal rules and procedures to ensure observance of any relevant regulations
- To monitor activities on a regular basis and in all areas of the organization to ensure that business is conducted in accordance with the regulations

Within these areas of responsibility there are many roles, including overseeing crime prevention within the organization by monitoring internal controls. Compliance's brief is a wide one covering everything from dealing and trading to marketing and awareness of the rules and regulations to which business is subjected. Compliance may be dealing with different procedures and processes in different business areas and needs to consider the internal controls as well as the external regulatory requirements.

Operations is responsible for the processes and procedures that are used in the function and it is these that will be monitored by compliance. Any changes to the regulatory environment needs to be reflected in the procedures and controls employed within the organization. Liaison between the two areas is therefore of paramount importance. Any changes to internal controls and/or procedures needs to be advised and dealt with jointly.

Many breaches of regulations occur because of out-of-date procedures, control failures or awareness problems. Compliance is the main contact between the organization and the external regulators and it is important that the communication between them and the Operations managers is good. Compliance will also be involved if there are problems that create breaches of regulation and managers will liaise over these with the regulator.

Audit

Audit's role is to review the processes, procedures and records to ensure that they have been correctly implemented and maintained. Although audit is in part a risk management process it is there to review the function, identify and report on any weaknesses it finds and make recommendations that should be considered by the Operations function in revamping procedures, processes and controls used. It cannot be expected to see every weakness and does not absolve the Operations managers from controlling risk in their function through adequate procedures.

Audit is a function that is carried out by independent external auditors as well as internally. Part of the external audits brief will be to report to the Regulator on how the organization is complying with the relevant regulations.

Compliance and audit are therefore monitoring and advising the Operations function and as such the relationship should be providing benefits to the business.

Issues with audit and compliance

Like Operations teams, compliance and audit are not always right. One significant problem is that the understanding within compliance and audit of the actual procedures and processes being employed is not always of a particularly high level. This can lead to mis-understandings and possibly loss of credibility among the Operations staff. As a result there is a danger that it will be perceived that any failure to adhere to rules or weaknesses in controls will either not be found or will be adequately explained away by the 'superior' knowledge of the Operations personnel.

Similarly, arguments can ensue about the effectiveness or otherwise of procedures and controls in relation to regulatory requirements, Operations personnel arguing that a control or procedure suggested by compliance is 'unworkable'. There is also the simple reluctance to admit to error and the consequences of being summoned to appear before the compliance officer. The result is that one or more members of the team may seek to hide the problem.

The combination of these points and others is this negative view of compliance and audit that so often pervades an organization, the Operations team being no exception. Yet without question both compliance and audit offer Operations much more in positives than negatives.

One of the first things that the Operations manager can do is to educate the team in what compliance and audit is really all about. In Chapter 5 we talked about the need to raise awareness of the whole business and to develop client, risk and business cultures. Part of that process will include explaining the role of compliance and audit and then explaining how they interact with the Operations function.

Raising awareness of the roles

What is the best approach? Most organizations run induction programmes for new recruits and this will include sessions on compliance and audit. This needs to be expanded so that the Operations team can relate them to the everyday functions they are involved with. To some extent money laundering, and the obligatory training requirement, begins this process.

Explaining the role of compliance

By including the role of compliance and audit in the developing of business, risk and client cultures, personnel should understand how the compliance with regulation and identification of weaknesses is crucial to the continuation of the business.

There are several ways to do this including providing copies of regulatory notices such as those issued by the FSA detailing the breaches of regulation and the punishment handed out. This will illustrate not only that a financial loss has probably occurred but also that the details of the firm's failures has been distributed publicly. By reinforcing the message with illustrations of how such a situation would damage the firm's reputation and cost it business in the future, the importance of the role of compliance can be made.

Another way of illustrating the importance of the interaction between Operations and compliance is to look at the client service provision and how identifying solutions to administrative and operational issues for clients can be rewarding for the business. Most organizations have regulatory reporting, record keeping, etc. To understand the requirements of the clients, including how they are affected by regulation as well as being fully aware of the regulation that applies in respect of the business the firms are doing for the client, is extremely important in a high-quality client service operation. Compliance can work together with the Operations teams by establishing regular briefings and disseminating information on regulatory updates, etc.

This all-round regulatory awareness can only help to develop a deeper awareness of the business itself and that in turn reduces the regulatory risk and simultaneously increases the possibility of developing solutions for clients that can be marketed.

Explaining the role of audit

Audit reviews the Operations function and provides an important independent look at the strengths and weaknesses of the processes, procedures and controls. Therefore it contributes to the overall effectiveness, efficiency and security of Operations.

As this is important for risk management as well as for regulatory and, indirectly, competitiveness, it is right that the Operations team should consider audit as a crucially important aid to a successful function.

By nature, audit can only review a small sample of the whole functionality of Operations, and therefore the Operations team must recognize that it cannot be relied on as the sole and primary control feature.

Seeking the views of audit when looking at the introduction of new products, processes and systems can be extremely useful. It saves the need to amend previously introduced procedures and removes the risk of operating with a weakness until the first audit after the implementation of new products, processes, systems and, of course, controls.

Summarizing relationships with compliance and audit

The most crucial issues are understanding and communication. Making sure that the Operations team understands the role of compliance and the regulator that compliance monitor must be part of the awareness programme the Operations manager introduces. There must also be a continuous programme of updating the team with key regulatory and compliance issues and encouraging the open-door approach to reporting possible breaches and problems.

Audit, like compliance, helps to protect the business and the positive image in the area that needs to be instilled in the team.

Essentially routine dialogue with both audit and compliance will gradually help the Operations manager to manage effectively. It is well worth it: after all, few things attract the attention of senior managers than a compliance problem or a critical audit report.

Chapter 8

The impact of change

Change is the hardest thing to manage. Most people are wary of change, irrespective of what they say. Change can and will get the adrenalin going and different people adapt to change in different ways. Some will take it in their stride, others will reluctantly accept change and others will oppose and fight it, sometimes vehemently. History is littered with groups fighting change, and to be fair some change is not good or necessary and people are entitled to voice their opposition. It is often the case that natural opposition to change is viewed as either militant obstruction or public-spirited heroism. In the UK the famous exploits of 'Swampy', a conservationist prepared to live in tunnels underground to prevent heavy equipment starting the process of building a contested road and later an airport runway, made him a quasi-national hero. Popular opposition is powerful and sometimes will certainly produce alterations to proposals if not curtail the project completely. It can also create prolonged delay in starting a project as the process of public consultations and enquiries are undertaken to hear the promoters' and objectors' points of view. The results can sometimes be highly damaging to the project, an example being the situation the UK found itself in when the Channel Tunnel rail link was completed. In France and Belgium new track had been constructed to take high-speed trains while in the UK the public enquiry into the proposed route for new track through the countryside of England was still going on. Result, super-fast train through France and Belgium and then a painfully slow train through England on old and crowded track. In the end the new route was approved but the delay and cost were colossal. Of course, those people and businesses affected by the proposed route had every right to oppose it but why did it take so long to decide the outcome in England compared to France and Belgium?

The kind of opposition to change that is seen in manufacturing and heavy industry is not so different from the kind of reaction some in Operations have to the proposal to change the way things are done, and, in particular, automation.

There are obviously reasons why the introduction of new working practices is viewed negatively. In industry it is about the probable loss of jobs, a change to processes or more work without a corresponding increase in pay. Trade unions will oppose such measures until they are modified or a satisfactory compensation for those affected is agreed with the management. This can produce strike action that can be costly and damaging to the business and even if the management get their way in the end the relations with their workforce is often at a very low point so that productivity is affected and more strike action is more likely.

The management of change is important if the business is not to suffer. In the Operations teams of businesses in the financial markets there is often little or no representation through an organized group such as a union. This is certainly the case in the UK although other European countries have different employment laws and rights for workers to be represented. Even where there is organized representation the nature of the business is such that militancy or strike action is unusual.

There is also the important point that change that is implemented without reasonable consultation, unless there is no choice for the manager, will have a high potential for teething troubles, loss of credibility and resentment. Balancing involvement and input with the need to introduce change within a timetable that suits the business is essential.

Change falls into two categories:

■ Changes driven by the industry
■ Changes driven by internal policies and management

The first category is likely to meet with little real resistance as it is usually perceived as beyond the control of the firm and the manager. Nevertheless, the resulting changes to procedures, system processes and jobs will not be without repercussions.

The second category, however, is more complex. Here the change is driven internally and by the supervisors and managers. It may be routine and of little sensitivity but equally it can be seen as driven from the business managers and a whole host of objections and difficulties can result, especially if jobs and working practices are involved.

The managers must therefore look at ways to effectively 'sell' the change by encompassing views and providing as much information and explanation as is possible. This can be done by following a procedure like the one shown in Table 8.1.

Table 8.1 'Selling' the change process

Change	Explain what it is and why it is policy including any alternatives that were considered
Objectives	How the change will impact
Implementation	How the change will be implemented including timetable
Training	Explain how personnel will be prepared for any new practices
Concerns	Identify possible concerns and address them
Discussion	Carry out a discussion programme with individuals/groups

By following this process the managers and supervisors can provide a business rationale as well as defining how and when the changes will take place.

Managing the actual implementations successfully is also vital and the coordination of this requires careful planning by the managers and supervisors. If we take, for instance, implementing the following changes.

1 Shortening UK settlement conventions to T+1
2 Using a CCP and netting

what are the primary issues in terms of change management?

Shortening UK settlement conventions to T+1

1 Government bonds and exchange-traded derivatives already settle T+1 so the main impact is in equity settlement
2 Most institutional business is already dematerialized via the CCP and settlement on due date is high (90%+)
3 Remaining certificated settlement will need to be phased out
4 Short sales will need stock borrowing facilities to settle
5 System data will need changing to reflect the changes

Using a CCP and netting

1 The use of a CCP will possibly involve new disciplines such as margin payments and collateral
2 Netting by the CCP rather than gross settlement would need system capabilities
3 Procedures and controls would need changing

These issues are going to affect businesses in different ways. An institutional client using a prime broker will have far less operational change to manage than a broker might experience. The basic situation is that the Operations team has to effect these changes if this is what the exchange/clearing house are going to implement. System and procedures are the principal concerns.

Now consider an internal situation such as the implementation of a new system and the combining of the securities and derivatives Operations teams. What are the primary issues?

New system implementation

1 The project will be, in all probability, of several months' duration
2 Critical timings and decisions will be needed about the introduction of the new system
3 Retraining programmes need to be decided
4 Procedures need review and updating
5 Parallel running and system testing will need to be carried out
6 Disruption to current workflow must be minimized
7 Operational risk will be higher
8 Resistance to change may become apparent

Merger of securities and derivatives Operations teams

1 A review of the skill sets and resource is needed
2 Benefits of the merger need explanation
3 Timetable needs to be agreed
4 Logistics like premises, systems, etc.
5 Identification of tasks, job specifications, supervision and manager roles
6 Assessment of resource
7 Retraining programmes
8 Procedures need review and updating
9 Resistance is possible
10 Job losses (if applicable) need managing
11 Implementation period must have heightened controls

The internal change process is potentially far harder and likely to meet resistance, and this is where the communication and involvement skills of the managers and supervisors are so important. However, it is not just managing the people but also dealing with the vitally important matters of reassessing procedures and controls, testing and sign-off and the retraining process. Managers have to rely on teamwork and crucially the support of the personnel to manage these types of major change projects. As the industry undergoes significant change in clearing and settlement as well as regulatory environments the need for the manager to be an effective change manager is essential.

Glossary

30/360 Also 360/360 or 30(E)/360. A day/year count convention assuming 30 days in each calendar month and a 'year' of 360 days; adjusted in America for certain periods ending on 31st-day of the month (and then sometimes known as 30(A)/360).

AAA The highest credit rating for a company or asset – the risk of default is negligible.

Accrued interest Interest due on a bond or other fixed income security that must be paid by the buyer of a security to its seller. Usual compensation: coupon rate of interest times elapsed days from prior interest payment date (i.e. coupon date) up to but not including settlement date.

Actual settlement date Date the transaction effectively settles in the clearing house (exchange of securities eventually against cash).

Add-on In capital adequacy calculations, the extra capital required to allow for the possibility of a deal moving into profit before a mark-to-market calculation is next made.

Affirmation Affirmation refers to the counterparty's agreement with the terms of the trade as communicated.

Agent One who executes orders for or otherwise acts on behalf of another (the principal) and is subject to its control and authority. The agent takes no financial risk and may receive a fee or commission.

Agent bank A commercial bank that provides services as per their instructions.

Allocation (give up) The process of moving the trade from the executing broker to the clearing broker in exchange-traded derivatives.

Amortization   Accounting procedure that gradually reduces the cost value of a limited life asset or intangible asset through periodic charges to income. The purpose of amortization is to reflect the resale or redemption value. Amortization also refers to the reduction of debt by regular payments of interest and principal to pay off a loan by maturity.

Annuity   For the recipient, an arrangement whereby the individual receives a pre-specified payment annually for a pre-specified number of years.

Ask price   Price at which a market-maker will sell stock. Also known as the offer price.

Assets   Everything of value that is owned or is due: fixed assets (cash, buildings and machinery) and intangible assets (patents and goodwill).

Assignment   The process by which the holder of a short option position is matched against a holder of a similar long option position who has exercised his right.

Authentication agent   A bank putting a signature on each physical bond to certify its genuineness prior to the distribution of the definitive bonds on the market.

Bank of England   The UK's central bank which undertakes policy decided by the Treasury and determines interest rates.

Bankers' acceptance   Short-term negotiable discount note, drawn on and accepted by banks which are obliged to pay the face value amount at maturity.

Bargain   Another word for a transaction or deal. It does not imply that a particularly favourable price was obtained.

Base currency   Currency chosen for reporting purposes.

Basis (gross)   The difference between the relevant cash instrument price and the futures price. Often used in the context of hedging the cash instrument.

Basis (value or net)   The difference between the gross basis and the carry.

Basis point (BP)   A change in the interest rate of one hundredth of one per cent (0.01%). One basis point is written as 0.01 when 1.0 represents 1%.

Basis risk The risk that the price or rate of one instrument or position might not move exactly in line with the price or rate of another instrument or position which is being used to hedge it.

BBA British Bankers' Association.

Bear Investor who believes prices will fall.

Bearer document Documents which state on them that the person in physical possession (the bearer) is the owner.

Benchmark bond The most recently issued and most liquid government bond.

Beneficial owner The underlying owner of a security who has paid for the stock and is entitled to the benefits of ownership.

Bid (a) The price or yield at which a purchaser is willing to buy a given security. (b) To quote a price or yield at which a purchaser is able to buy a given security.

Bilateral netting A netting system in which all trades executed on the same date in the same security between the same counter-parties are grouped and netted to one final delivery versus payment.

Bill of exchange A money market instrument.

BIS Bank for International Settlements.

Block trade A purchase or sale of a large number of shares or dollar value of bonds normally much more than what constitutes a round lot in the market in question.

Bond A certificate of debt, generally long-term, under the terms of which an issuer contracts, *inter alia*, to pay the holder a fixed principal amount on a stated future date and, usually, a series of interest payments during its life.

Bonus issue A free issue of shares to a company's existing shareholders. No money changes hands and the share price falls pro rata. It is a cosmetic exercise to make the shares more marketable. Also known as a capitalization or scrip issue.

Book entry transfer System of recording ownership of securities by computer where the owners do not receive a certificate. Records are kept (and altered) centrally in 'the book'.

Books closed day Last date for the registration of shares or bonds for the payment of the next.

Break   A term used for any out-of-balance condition. A money break means that debits and credits are not equal. A trade break means that some information such as that from a contra broker is missing to complete that trade.

Broker/dealer   Any member firm of the Stock Exchange except the specialists which are GEMMs and IDBs.

Broken date   A maturity date other than the standard ones normally quoted.

Broken period   A period other than the standard ones normally quoted.

Broking   The activity of representing a client as agent and charging commission for doing so.

Bull   Investor who believes prices will rise.

Buying in   The action taken by a broker failing to receive delivery of securities from a counterparty on settlement date to purchase these securities in the open market.

Call deposits   Deposits which can be called (or withdrawn) at the option of the lender (and in some cases the borrower) after a specified period. The period is short, usually one or two days, and interest is paid at prevailing short-term rates (call account).

Call option   An option that gives the seller the right, but not the obligation, to buy a specified quantity of the underlying asset at a fixed price, on or before a specified date. The buyer of a call option has the obligation (because they have bought the right) to make delivery of the underlying asset if the option is exercised by the seller.

Callable bond   A bond that the issuer has the right to redeem prior to maturity by paying some specified call price.

Capital adequacy   Requirement for firms conducting investment business to have sufficient funds.

Capital markets   A term used to describe the means by which large amounts of money (capital) are raised by companies, governments and other organizations for long-term use and the subsequent trading of the instruments issued in recognition of such capital.

Capitalization issue   *See* **Bonus issue**.

CASCADE Name of the settlement system used by Clearstream for German equity settlement.

Cash market A term used to describe the market where the cash asset trades, or the underlying market when talking about derivatives.

Cash sale A transaction on the floor of the stock exchange which calls for delivery of the securities that same day. In 'regular way' trades, the seller delivers securities on the fifth business day.

Cash settlement In the money market a transaction is said to be made for cash settlement if the securities purchased are delivered against payment on the same day the trade is made.

Central securities depository An organization which holds securities in either immobilized or dematerialized form thereby enabling transactions to be processed by book entry transfer. Also provides securities administration services.

Certificate of deposit A money market instrument.

CFTC The Commodities and Futures Commission, (United States).

Chaps Clearing House Automated Payment System – clearing system for sterling and Euro payments between banks.

Cheapest to deliver The cash security that provides the lowest cost (largest profit) to the arbitrage trader; the cheapest to deliver instrument is used to price the futures contract.

Clean price The total price of a bond less accrued interest.

Clearance The process of determining accountability for the exchange of money and securities between counterparties to a trade: clearance creates statements of obligation for securities and/or funds due.

Clearance broker A broker who will handle the settlement of securities related transactions for himself or another broker. Sometimes small brokerage firms may not clear for themselves and therefore employ the services of an outside clearing broker.

Clearing The centralized process whereby transacted business is recorded and positions are maintained.

Clearing house Company that acts as central counterparty for the settlement of stock exchange transactions. For example, on TD,

Broker X sold 100, 300 and 500 securities ABC and purchased 50 and 200 units of the same issue. The clearing system will net the transactions and debit X with 650 units ($-900 + 250 = 650$) against the total cash amount. This enables reduction of the number of movements and thus the costs.

Clearing organization   The clearing organization acts as the guarantor of the performance and settlement of contracts that are traded on an exchange.

Clearing system   System established to clear transactions.

Clearstream   CSD and clearing house based in Luxembourg and Frankfurt.

Closing day   In a new bond issue, the day when securities are delivered against payment by syndicate members participating in the offering.

Closing trade   A bought or sold trade which is used to partly offset an open position, to reduce it or to fully offset it and close it.

CMO   Central Moneymarkets Office – clearing house and depository for UK money markets.

Collateral   An acceptable asset used to cover a margin requirement.

Commercial paper   A money market instrument.

Commission   Charge levied by a firm for agency broking.

Commodity futures   These comprise five main categories: agriculturals (e.g. wheat and potatoes); softs (e.g. coffee and cocoa); precious metals (e.g. gold and silver); non-ferrous metals (e.g. copper and lead); and energies (e.g. oil and gas).

Common stock   Securities which represent ownership in a corporation. The two most important common stockholder rights are the voting right and dividend right. Common stockholders' claims on corporate assets are subordinate to those of bondholders, preferred stockholders and general creditors.

Compliance officer   Person appointed within an authorized firm to be responsible for ensuring compliance with the rules.

Compound interest   Interest calculated on the assumption that interest amounts will be received periodically and can be reinvested (usually at the same rate).

Conduct of Business Rules Rules required by FSA 1986 to dictate how firms conduct their business. They deal mainly with the relationship between firm and client.

Conflicts of interest Circumstances that arise where a firm has an investment which could encourage it not to treat its clients favourably. The more areas in which a firm is involved, the greater the number of potential conflicts.

Confirm An agreement for each individual OTC transaction which has specific terms.

Continuous net settlement Extends multilateral netting to handle failed trades brought forward. *See* **Multilateral netting**.

Contract The standard unit of trading for futures and options. It is also commonly referred to as a 'lot'.

Contract for difference Contract designed to make a profit or avoid a loss by reference to movements in the price of an item. The underlying item cannot change hands.

Contract note Legal documentation sent by a securities house to clients providing details of a transaction completed on their behalf.

Conversion premium The effective extra cost of buying shares through exercising a convertible bond compared with buying the shares directly in the market. Usually expressed as a percentage of the current market price of the shares.

Conversion price The normal value of a convertible which may be exchanged for one share.

Conversion ratio The number of shares into which a given amount (e.g. £100 or $1000) of the nominal value of a convertible can be converted.

Convertible bond Security (usually a bond or preferred stock) that can be exchanged for other securities, usually common stock of the same issuer, at the option of the holder and under certain conditions.

Convertible currency A currency that is freely convertible into another currency. Currencies for which domestic exchange control legislation specifically allows conversion into other currencies.

Corporate action One of many possible capital restructuring changes or similar actions taken by the company, which may have an impact on the market price of its securities, and which may require the shareholders to make certain decisions.

Corporate debt securities   Bonds or commercial papers issued by private corporations.

Correlation   Refers to the degree to which fluctuations of one variable are similar to those of another.

Cost of carry   The net running cost of holding a position (which may be negative), e.g. the cost of borrowing cash to buy a bond, less the coupon earned on the bond while holding it.

Counterparty   A trade can take place between two or more counterparties. Usually one party to a trade refers to its trading partners as counterparties.

Coupon   Generally, the nominal annual rate of interest expressed as a percentage of the principal value. The interest is paid to the holder of a fixed income security by the borrower. The coupon is generally paid annually, semi-annually or, in some cases quarterly depending on the type of security.

Credit risk   The risk that a borrower, or a counterparty to a deal, or the issuer of a security, will default on repayment or not deliver its side of the deal.

CREST   The organization in the UK that holds UK and Irish company shares in dematerialized form and clears and settles trades in UK and Irish company shares.

CRESTCo   Organization which owns CREST.

CREST member   A participant within CREST who holds stock in stock accounts in CREST and whose name appears on the share register. A member is their own user.

CREST sponsored member   A participant within CREST who holds stock in stock accounts in CREST and whose name appears on the share register. Unlike a member, a sponsored member is not their own user. The link to CREST is provided by another user who sponsors the sponsored member.

CREST user   A participant within CREST who has an electronic link to CREST.

Cross-border trading   Trading which takes place between persons or entities from different countries.

Cum-dividend   With dividend.

Cumulative preference share   If the company fails to pay a preference dividend the entitlement to the dividend accumulates and the arrears of preference dividend must be paid before any ordinary dividend.

Currency exposure   Currency exposure exists if assets are held or income earned, in one currency while liabilities are denominated in another currency. The position is exposed to changes in the relative values of the two currencies such that the cost of the liabilities may be increased or the value of the assets or earning decreased.

CUSIP   The Committee on Uniform Securities Identification Procedures, the body which established a consistent securities numbering system in the United States.

Custodian   Institution holding securities in safekeeping for a client. A custodian also offers different services to its clients (settlement, portfolio services, etc.)

Customer-non-private   Customer who is assumed to understand the workings of the investment world and therefore receives little protection from the Conduct of Business Rules.

Customer-private   Customer who is assumed to be financially unsophisticated and therefore receives more protection from the Conduct of Business Rules.

Day count fraction   The proportion of a year by which an interest rate is multiplied in order to calculate the amount accrued or payable.

Dealer   Individual or firm that acts as principal in all transactions, buying for their own account.

Default   Failure to perform on a futures contract, either cash settlement or physical settlement.

Deliverable basket   The list of securities which meets the delivery standards of futures contracts.

Delivery   The physical movement of the underlying asset on which the derivative is based from seller to buyer.

Delivery versus payment   Settlement where transfer of the security and payment for that security occur simultaneously.

Dematerialized (form)   Circumstances where securities are held in a book entry transfer system with no certificates.

Depository receipts   Certificate issued by a bank in a country to represent shares of a foreign corporation issued in a foreign country. It entitles the holder to dividends and capital gains. They trade and pay dividend in the currency of the country of issuance of the certificate.

Depository Trust Company (DTC)   A US central securities depository through which members may arrange deliveries of securities between each other through electronic debit and credit entries without the physical delivery of the securities. DTC is industry-owned with the NYSE as the majority owner and is a member of the Federal Reserve System.

Derivative   A financial instrument whose value is dependent upon the value of an underlying asset.

Dirty price   The total price of a bond including accrued interest.

Disclaimer   A notice or statement intending to limit or avoid potential legal liability.

Deutsche Börse   The German Stock Exchange.

Dividend   Distribution of profits made by a company if it chooses to do so.

Dividend per share   Indicated annual dividend based on the most recently announced quarterly dividend times four plus any additional dividends to be paid during the current fiscal year.

Dividend yield   The dividend expressed as a percentage of the share price.

DK   Don't Know. Applies to a securities transaction pending settlement where fundamental data are missing which prevents the receiving party from accepting delivery.

Domestic bond   Bond issued in the country of the issuer, in its country and according to the regulations of that country.

DTC   Depository Trust Company – CSD for shares in the USA.

ECB   European Central Bank.

ECSDA   European Central Securities Depository Association.

EFP   Exchange of futures for physical. Common in the energy markets. A physical deal priced on the futures markets.

EUCLID   Communications system operated by Euroclear.

EUREX German–Swiss derivatives exchange created by the merger of the German (DTB) and Swiss (SOFFEX) exchanges.

EURONEXT A Pan-European exchange incorporating the Dutch, French and Belgium Exchanges and Liffe.

Earnings per share (EPS) The total profit of a company divided by the number of shares in issue.

Equity A common term to describe stocks or shares.

Equity/stock options Contracts based on individual equities or shares. On exercise of the option the specified amount of shares are exchanged between the buyer and the seller through the clearing organization.

E-T-D This is the common term which is used to describe exchange-traded derivatives which are the standardized products. It also differentiates products which are listed on an exchange as opposed to those offered Over-The-Counter.

EURIBOR A measure of the average cost of funds over the whole euro area based on a panel of 57 banks.

Eurobond An interest-bearing security issued across national borders, usually issued in a currency other than that of the issuer's home country.

Euroclear A book-entry clearing facility for most Eurocurrency and foreign securities. It is linked to EURONEXT.

European style option An option which can only be exercised on the expiry day.

Exception-based processing Transaction processing where straightforward items are processed automatically, allowing staff to concentrate on the items which are incorrect or not straight-forward.

Execution and clearing agreement An agreement signed between the client and the clearing broker. This agreement sets out the terms by which the clearing broker will conduct business with the client.

Exchange Marketplace for trading.

Exchange delivery settlement price (EDSP) The price determined by the exchange for physical delivery of the underlying instrument or cash settlement.

Exchange-owned clearing organization   Exchange- or member-owned clearing organizations are structured so that the clearing members each guarantee each other with the use of a members' default fund and additional funding such as insurance, with no independent guarantee.

Exchange rate   The rate at which one currency can be exchanged for another.

Ex-date   Date on or after which a sale of securities is executed without the right to receive dividends or other entitlements.

Ex-dividend   Thirty-seven days before interest payment is due gilt-edged stocks are made 'ex-dividend'. After a stock has become 'ex-dividend', a buyer of stock purchases it without the right to receive the next (pending) interest payment.

Execution   The action of trading in the markets.

Execution and clearing agreement   An agreement signed between the client and the clearing broker. This sets out the terms by which the clearing broker will conduct business with the client.

Execution only or give-up agreement   Tripartite agreement which is signed by the executing broker, the clearing broker and the client. This sets out the terms by which the clearing broker will accept business on behalf of the client.

Exercise   The process by which the holder of an option may take up their right to buy or sell the underlying asset.

Exercise price (or strike price)   The fixed price, per share or unit, at which an option conveys the right to call (purchase) or put (sell) the underlying shares or units.

Expiry date   The last date on which an option holder can exercise their right. After this date an option is deemed to lapse or be abandoned.

Face value   The value of a bond, note, mortgage or other security that appears on the face of the issue, unless the value is otherwise specified by the issuing company. Face value is ordinarily the amount the issuing company promises to pay at maturity. It is also referred to as par or nominal value.

Failed transaction   A securities transaction that does not settle on time; i.e. the securities and/or cash are not exchanged as agreed on the settlement date.

Final settlement The completion of a transaction when the delivery of all components of a trade is performed.

Financial futures/options contracts Financial futures is a term used to describe futures contracts based on financial instruments such as currencies, debt instruments and financial indices.

Financial Services Authority (FSA) The agency designated by the Treasury to regulate investment business as required by FSA 1986 and then FSMA 2000. It is the main regulator of the financial sector and was formerly called the Securities and Investments Board (SIB). It assumed its full powers on 1 December 2001.

First notice day The first day that the holders of short positions can give notification to the exchange/clearing house that they wish to effect delivery.

Fiscal agent A commercial bank appointed by the borrower to undertake certain duties related to the new issue, such as assisting the payment of interest and principal, redeeming bonds or coupons, handling taxes, replacement of lost or damaged securities, destruction of coupons and bonds once payments have been made.

Fixed income Interest on a security which is calculated as a constant specified percentage of the principal amount and paid at the end of specified interest periods, usually annually or semi-annually, until maturity.

Fixed rate A borrowing or investment where the interest or coupon paid is fixed throughout the arrangement. In a FRA or coupon swap, the fixed rate is the fixed interest rate paid by one party to the other, in return for a floating-rate receipt (i.e. an interest rate that is to be refixed at some future time or times).

Fixed-rate borrowing This establishes the interest rate that will be paid throughout the life of the loan.

Flat position A position which has been fully closed out and no liability to make or take delivery exists.

Floating rate A borrowing or investment where the interest or coupon paid changes throughout the arrangement in line with some reference rate such as LIBOR. In a FRA or coupon swap, the floating rate is the floating interest rate (i.e. an interest rate that is to be refixed at some future time or times) paid by one party to the other, in return for a fixed-rate receipt.

Floating-rate note (FRN)   Bond where each interest payment is made at the current or average market levels, often by reference to LIBOR.

Foreign bond   Bond issued in a domestic market in the domestic currency and under the domestic rules of issuance by a foreign issuer (ex. Samurai bonds are bonds issued by issuers of other countries on the Japanese market).

Forex   Abbreviation for foreign exchange (currency trading).

Forward delivery   Transactions which involve a delivery date in the future.

Forward-rate agreements (FRAs)   An agreement where the client can fix the rate of interest that will be applied to a notional loan or deposit, drawn or placed on an agreed date in the future, for a specified term.

Forwards   These are very similar to futures contracts but they are not mainly traded on an exchange. They are not marked to market daily but settled only on the delivery date.

FSA   Financial Services Authority.

FT-SE 100 index   Main UK share index based on 100 leading shares.

Fund manager   An organization that invests money on behalf of someone else.

Futures   An agreement to buy or sell an asset at a certain time in the future for a certain price.

Gearing   The characteristic of derivatives which enables a far greater reward for the same, or much smaller, initial outlay. It is the ratio of exposure to investment outlay, and is also known as leverage.

Gilt   Domestic sterling-denominated long-term bond backed by the full faith and credit of the UK and issued by the Treasury.

Gilt-edged market-makers (GEMMs)   A firm that is a market maker in gilts. Also known as a primary dealer.

Gilt-edged security   UK government borrowing.

Give-up   The process of giving a trade to a third party who will undertake the clearing and settlement of the trade.

Global clearing The channelling of the settlement of all futures and options trades through a single counterparty or through a number of counterparties geographically located.

Global custodian Institution that safekeeps, settles and performs processing of income collection, tax reclaim, multicurrency reporting, cash management, foreign exchange, corporate action and proxy monitoring etc. for clients' securities in all required marketplaces.

Global depository receipt (GDR) A security representing shares held in custody in the country of issue.

Good delivery Proper delivery of certificates that are negotiable and complete in terms of documentation or information.

Gross A position which is held with both the bought and sold trades kept open.

GSCC Government Securities Clearing Corporation – clearing organization for US Treasury securities.

Guaranteed bond Bonds on which the principal or income or both are guaranteed by another corporation or parent company in case of default by the issuing corporation.

Haircut The discount applied to the value of collateral used to cover margins.

Hedging A trading method which is designed to reduce or mitigate risk. Reducing the risk of a cash position in the futures instrument to offset the price movement of the cash asset. A broader definition of hedging includes using futures as a temporary substitute for the cash position.

Holder A person who has bought an open derivatives contract.

Immobilization The storage of securities certificates in a vault in order to eliminate physical movement of certificates/documents in transfer of ownership.

Independent clearing organization The independent organization is quite separate from the actual members of the exchange, and will guarantee to each member the performance of the contracts by having them registered in the organization's name.

Initial margin The deposit which the clearing house calls as protection against a default of a contract. It is returnable to the clearing member once the position is closed. The level is subject to changes in line with market conditions.

Institutional investor An institution which is usually investing money on behalf of others. Examples are mutual funds and pension funds.

Interest rate futures Based on a debt instrument such as a government bond or a Treasury bill as the underlying product and require the delivery of a bond or bill to fulfil the contract.

Interest rate swap An agreement to exchange interest related payments in the same currency from fixed rate into floating rate (or vice versa) or from one type of floating rate to another.

Interim dividend Dividend paid part-way through a year in advance of the final dividend.

International depository receipt (IDR) Receipt of shares of a foreign corporation held in the vaults of a depository bank. The receipt entitles the holder to all dividends and capital gains. Dividends and capital gains are converted to local currency as part of the service. IDRs allow investors to purchase foreign shares without having to involve themselves in foreign settlements and currency conversion.

International equity An equity of a company based outside the UK but traded internationally.

International petroleum exchange (IPE) Market for derivatives of petrol and oil products.

International securities identification number (ISIN) A coding system developed by the ISO for identifying securities. ISINs are designated to create one unique worldwide number for any security. It is a 12-digit alphanumeric code.

Interpolation The estimation of a price or rate, usually for a broken date, from two other rates or prices, each of which is for a date either side of the required date.

Intra-day margin An extra margin call which the clearing organization can call during the day when there is a very large movement up or down in the price of the contract.

Intrinsic value The amount by which an option is in-the-money.

Investment services directive (ISD) European Union Directive imposing common standards on investment business.

Investments Items defined in the FSA 1986 to be regulated by it. Includes shares, bonds, options, futures, life assurance and pensions.

Invoice amount The amount calculated under the formula specified by the futures exchange which will be paid in settlement of the delivery of the underlying asset.

IOSCO International Organization of Securities Commissions.

IPMA International Primary Markets Association.

Irredeemable gilt A gilt with no fixed date for redemption. Investors receive interest indefinitely.

ISDA International Swaps and Derivatives Association, previously known as the International Swap Dealers Association. Many market participants use ISDA documentation.

ISMA International Securities Markets Association.

ISSA The International Securities Services Association.

Issuer Legal entity that issues and distributes securities.

Issuing agent Agent (e.g. bank) who puts original issues out for sale.

JASDEC Japan Securities Depository Centre – the CSD for Japan.

JSCC Japan Securities Clearing Corporation – clearing organization in Japan.

Last notice day The final day that notification of delivery of a futures contract will be possible. On most exchanges all outstanding short futures contracts will be automatically delivered to open long positions.

Last trading day Often the day preceding last notice day which is the final opportunity for holders of long positions to trade out of their positions and avoid ultimate delivery.

LCH London Clearing House.

Leverage The magnification of gains and losses by only paying for part of the underlying value of the instrument or asset; the smaller the amount of funds invested, the greater the leverage. It is also known as gearing.

LIBID   The London inter-bank bid rate. The rate at which one bank will lend to another.

LIBOR   The London inter-bank offered rate. It is the rate used when one bank borrows from another bank. It is the benchmark used to price many capital market and derivative transactions.

LIFFE   London International Financial Futures and Options Exchange.

Liquidity   A liquid asset is one that can be converted easily and rapidly into cash without a substantial loss of value. In the money market, a security is said to be liquid if the spread between bid and asked price is narrow and reasonable size can be done at those quotes.

Liquidity risk   The risk that a bank may not be able to close out a position because the market is illiquid.

Listed securities   Securities listed on a stock exchange are tradeable on this exchange.

Loan stock   *See* **Bond**.

London Inter-Bank Offered Rate (LIBOR)   Rate at which banks lend to each other which is often used as the benchmark for floating rate notes (FRNs).

London International Financial Futures and Options Exchange (LIFFE)   Market for trading in bond, interest rate, FT-SE 100 index and FTSE Mid 250 index, futures, plus equity options and soft commodity derivatives.

London Metal Exchange (LME)   Market for trading in derivatives of metals such as copper, tin, zinc, etc.

London Stock Exchange (LSE)   Market for trading in securities. Formerly known as the International Stock Exchange of the UK and Republic of Ireland or ISE.

Long   A bought position in a derivative which is held open.

Long-dated   Gilts with more than 15 years until redemption.

Long position   Refers to an investor's account in which he has more shares of a specific security than he needs to meet his settlement obligations.

Lot   The common term used to describe the standard unit of trading for futures and options. It is also referred to as a 'contract'.

Mandatory event   A corporate action which affects the securities without giving any choice to the security holder.

Margin   *Initial margin* is collateral placed by one party with a counterparty or clearing house at the time of a deal, against the possibility that the market price will move against the first party, thereby leaving the counterparty with a credit risk. *Variation margin* is a payment made, or collateral transferred, from one party to the other because the market price of the transaction or of collateral has changed. Variation margin payment is either in effect a settlement of profit/loss (for example, in the case of a futures contract) or the reduction of credit exposure. In a loan, margin is the extra interest above a benchmark such as LIBOR required by a lender to compensate for the credit risk of that particular borrower.

Mark-to-market   The process of revaluing an OTC or exchange-traded product each day. It is the difference between the closing price on the previous day against the current closing price. For exchange traded products this is referred to as variation margin.

Market   Description of any organization or facility through which items are traded. All exchanges are markets.

Market counterparty   A person dealing as agent or principal with the broker and involved in the same nature of investment business as the broker. This also includes fellow members of the FSA or trading members of an investment exchange for those products only where they are members.

Market-maker   A trader who works for an organization such as an investment bank. They quote bids and offers in the market and are normally under an obligation to make a price in a certain number of contracts. They create liquidity in the contract by offering to buy or sell.

Market price   In the case of a security, the market price is usually considered as the last reported price at which the stock or bond has been sold.

Market risk   Also position risk. The risk that the market value of a position falls.

Market value   The price at which a security is trading and could presumably be purchased or sold.

Master agreement   This agreement is for OTC transactions and is signed between the client and the broker. It covers the basic terms under which the client and broker wish to transact business. Each individual trade has a separate individual agreement with specific terms known as a confirm.

Matching (comparison)   Another term for comparison (or checking); a matching system to compare trades and ensure that both sides of trade correspond.

Maturity   The date on which the principal or nominal value of a bond becomes due and payable in full to the holder.

Medium dated   Gilts due to be redeemed within the next seven to fifteen years.

Model risk   The risk that the computer model used by a bank for valuation or risk assessment is incorrect or misinterpreted.

Modified following   The convention that if a settlement date in the future falls on a non-business day, the settlement date will be moved to the next following business day, unless this moves it to the next month, in which case the settlement date is moved back to the last previous business day.

Money market   The market for the purchase and sale of short-term financial instruments. Short term is usually defined as less than one year.

Money rate of return   Annual return as a percentage of asset value.

MOF   The Ministry of Finance (Japan).

Multilateral netting   Trade between several counterparties in the same security are netted such that each counterparty makes only one transfer of cash or securities to another party or to a central clearing system. Handles only transactions due for settlement on the same day.

Mutual collateralization   The deposit of collateral by both counterparties to a transaction.

NASDAQ   National Association of Securities Dealers Automated Quotation system.

Netting   Trading partners offset their positions thereby reducing the number of positions for settlement. Netting can be *bilateral*, *multilateral* or *continuous net settlement*.

Net asset value (NAV)   In mutual funds, the market value of the fund share. It is common practice for an investment trust to compute its assets daily, or even twice a day, by totalling the closing market value of all securities and assets (i.e. cash) owned. All liabilities are deducted, and the balance is divided by the number of shares outstanding. The resulting figure is the net asset value per share.

Net present value (NPV)   The net total of several present values (arising from cashflows at different future dates) added together, some of which may be positive and some negative.

Nil paid rights price   Ex-rights price less the subscription price.

Nominal amount   Value stated on the face of a security (principal value, par value). Securities processing: number of securities to deliver/receive.

Nominal value of a bond   The value at which the capital, or principal, of a bond will be redeemed by the issuer. Also called par value.

Nominal value of a share   The minimum price at which a share can be issued. Also called par value.

Nominee   An organization that acts as the named owner of securities on behalf of a different beneficial owner who remains anonymous to the company.

Non-callable   Cannot be redeemed by the issuer for a stated period of time from date of issue.

Non-clearing member   A member of an exchange who does not undertake to settle their derivatives business. This type of member must appoint a clearing member to register all their trades at the clearing organization.

Non-cumulative preference share   If the company fails to pay a preference dividend the entitlement to the dividend is simply lost. There is no accumulation.

Non-private customer   A person who is not a private customer or who has requested to be treated as a non-private customer.

Nostro reconciliation   Checking the entries shown on the bank's nostro account statement with the bank's internal records (the accounting ledgers) to ensure that they correspond exactly.

Note   Bonds issued with a relatively short maturity are often called notes.

Notional   Contracts for differences require a notional principal amount on which settlement can be calculated.

Novation   The process where registered trades are cancelled with the clearing members and substituted by two new ones – one between the clearing house and the clearing member seller, the other between the clearing house and the clearing member buyer.

NSCC   National Securities Clearing Corporation – clearing organization for US shares.

OASYS   Trade confirmation system for US brokers operated by Thomson Financial Services.

Obligation netting   An arrangement to transfer only the net amount (of cash or a security) due between two or more parties, rather than transfer all amounts between the parties on a gross basis.

Off-balance sheet   A transaction whose principal amount is not shown on the balance sheet because it is a contingent liability or settled as a contract for differences.

Offer price   The price at which a trader or market-maker is willing to sell a contract.

Offshore   Relates to locations outside the controls of domestic monetary, exchange and legislative authorities. Offshore may not necessarily be outside the national boundaries of a country. In some countries, certain banks or other institutions may be granted offshore status and thus be exempt from all or specific controls or legislation.

Omnibus account   Account containing the holdings of more than one client.

On-balance sheet   A transaction whose principal amount is shown on the balance sheet.

On-line   Processing which is executed via an interactive input onto a PC or stationary terminal connected to a processing centre.

Open outcry   The style of trading whereby traders face each other in a designated area such as a pit and shout or call their respective bids and offers. Hand signals are also used to communicate. It is governed by exchange rules.

Open interest   The number of contracts both bought and sold which remain open for delivery on an exchange. Important indicator for liquidity.

Open position   The number of contracts which have not been off-set at the clearing organization by the close of business.

Opening trade   A bought or sold trade which is held open to create a position.

Operational risk   The risk of losses resulting from inadequate systems and control, human errors or management failings.

Option   An option is in the case of the *buyer*; the right, but not the obligation, to take (call) or make (put) for delivery of the underlying product and in the case of the *seller*; the obligation to make or take delivery of the underlying product.

Option premium   The sum of money paid by the buyer for acquiring the right of the option. It is the sum of money received by the seller for incurring the obligation, having sold the rights, of the option. It is the sum of the intrinsic value and the time value.

Optional dividend   Dividend that can be paid either in cash or in stock. The shareholders entitled to the dividend make the choice.

Options on futures   These have the same characteristics as an option, the difference being that the underlying product is either a long or short futures contract. Premium is not exchanged, the contracts are marked to market each day.

Order-driven market   A stock market where brokers acting on behalf of clients match trades with each other either on the trading floor of the exchange or through a central computer system.

Out-of-pocket expenses   Market charges which are charged to the client without taking any profit.

Out-trade   A trade which has been incorrectly matched on the floor of an exchange.

Over-the-counter (OTC)   A one-to-one agreement between two counterparties where the specifications of the product are completely flexible and non-standardized.

Over-the-counter trading   Trading made outside a stock exchange.

Pair off   Back-to-back trade between two parties where settlement occurs only by exchanging the cash difference between the two parties.

Par value   *See* **Nominal value**.

Pari passu   Without partiality. Securities that rank *pari passu*, rank equally with each other.

Paying agent   A bank which handles payment of interest and dividends on behalf of the issuer of a security.

Payment date   Date on which a dividend or an interest payment is scheduled to be paid.

Perpetual bond   A bond which has no redemption date.

Portfolio   List of investments held by an individual or company, or list of loans made by a bank or financial institution.

Premium   An option premium is the amount paid upfront by the purchaser of the option to the writer.

Present value   The amount of money which needs to be invested (or borrowed) now at a given interest rate in order to achieve exactly a given cashflow in the future, assuming compound reinvestment (or refunding) of any interest payments received (or paid) before the end.

Pre-settlement   Checks and procedures undertaken immediately after execution of a trade prior to settlement.

Principal protected product   An investment whose maturity value is guaranteed to be at least the principal amount invested initially.

Principal-to-principal market   A market where the clearing house recognizes only the clearing member as one entity, and not the underlying clients of the clearing member.

Principal trading   When a member firm of the London Stock Exchange buys stock from or sells stock to a non-member.

Principal value   That amount inscribed on the face of a security and exclusive of interest or premium. It is the one used in the computation of interest due on such a security.

Private customer   An individual person who is not acting in the course of carrying on investment business.

Proprietary trader   A trader who deals for an organization such as an investment bank taking advantage of short-term price movements as well as taking long-term views on whether the market will move up or down.

Put option An option that gives the buyer the right, but not the obligation, to sell a specified quantity of the underlying asset at a fixed price, on or before a specified date. The seller of a put option has the obligation (because they have sold the right) to take delivery of the underlying asset if the option is exercised by the buyer.

Quote driven Dealing system where some firms accept the responsibility to quote buying and selling prices.

Range forward A forward outright with two forward rates, where settlement takes place at the higher forward rate if the spot rate at maturity is higher than that, at the lower forward rate if the spot rate at maturity is lower than that, or at the spot rate at maturity otherwise.

RCH Recognized clearing house under FSMA 2000.

Real-time gross settlement (RTGS) Gross settlement system where trades are settled continuously through the processing day.

Realized profit Profit which has arisen from a real sale.

Recognized investment exchange (RIE) Status required by FSMA 2000 for exchanges in the UK.

Reconciliation The comparison of a person's records of cash and securities position with records held by another party and the investigation and resolution of any discrepancies between the two sets of records.

Record date The date on which a securities holder must hold the securities in order to receive an income or entitlement.

Redemption The purchase and cancellation of outstanding securities through a cash payment to the holder.

Redemption price A price at which bonds may be redeemed, or called, at the issuer's option, prior to maturity (often with a slight premium).

Registered bond A bond whose owner is registered with the issuer or its registrar.

Registered title Form of ownership of securities where the owner's name appears on a register maintained by the company.

Registrar An official of a company who maintains its share register.

Registrar of companies Government department responsible for keeping records of all companies.

Replacement cost The mark-to-market loss which would be incurred if it were necessary to undertake a new transaction to replace an existing one, because the existing counterparty defaulted.

Repurchase agreement (repo) Borrowing funds by providing a government security for collateral and promising to 'repurchase' the security at the end of the agreed upon time period. The associated interest rate is the 'repo-rate'.

Reputational risk The risk that an organization's reputation will be damaged.

RIE Recognized investment exchange under FSA 1986.

Rights issue Offer of shares made to existing shareholders.

Right of offset Where positions and cash held by the clearing organization in different accounts for a member are allowed to be netted.

Risk warning Document that must be despatched and signed by private customers before they deal in traded options.

Roll-over A LIBOR fixing on a new tranche of loan, or transfer of a futures position to the next delivery month.

Rolling settlement System used in most countries including England. Bargains are settled a set number of days after being transacted.

Safekeeping Holding of securities on behalf of clients. They are free to sell at any time.

SCL Settlement organization and custodian of Spanish securities.

Scrip dividends Scrip dividends options provide shareholders with the choice of receiving dividend entitlements in the form of cash, shares or a combination of both. The amount of stocks to be distributed under a scrip option is calculated by dividing the cash dividend amount by the average market price over a recent period of time.

Scrip issue *See* **Bonus issue**.

SEATS Plus An order-driven system used on the London Stock Exchange for securities which do not attract at least two firms of market-makers and for all AIM securities.

Secondary market   Marketplace for trading in existing securities. The price at which they are trading has no direct effect on the company's fortunes but is a reflection of investors' perceptions of the company.

Securities   Bonds and equities.

Securities house   General term covering any type of organization involved in securities although usually reserved for the larger firms.

Securities lending   Loan of securities by an investor to another (usually a broker–dealer), usually to cover a short sale.

Securities and futures authority (SFA)   Prior to the FSA assuming its full powers, it was the SRO responsible for regulating securities and futures firms.

Securities and investments board (SIB)   Former name of the Financial Services Authority.

SEDOL   Stock Exchange Daily Official List, a securities numbering system assigned by the International Stock Exchange in London.

Segregated account   Account in which there is only the holdings of one client.

Segregation of funds   Where the client's assets are held separately from those assets belonging to the member firm.

Self-regulating organizations (SROs)   Bodies which receive their status from FSA and are able to regulate sectors of the financial services industry. Membership of an SRO provides authorization.

SEQUAL   The checking system used for international equities.

SETS   London Stock Exchange Trading System.

Settlement   The fulfilment of the contractual commitments of transacted business.

Settlement date   The date on which a trade is cleared by delivery of securities against funds (actual settlement date, contractual settlement date).

Share option   A right sold to an investor conferring the option to buy or sell shares of a particular company at a predetermined price and within a specified time limit.

Short   A sold position in a derivative which is held open.

Short coupons   Bonds or notes with a short current maturity.

Short cover   The purchase of a security that has been previously sold short. The purpose is to return securities that were borrowed to make a delivery.

Short-dated gilt   Gilts due to be redeemed within the next seven years, according to the LSE (FT states up to 5 years).

Short sale   The sale of securities not owned by the seller in the expectation that the price of these securities will fall or as part of an arbitrage.

Short selling   Selling stock that you do not own.

Short-term security   Generally an obligation maturing in less than one year.

SICOVAM   CSD for French corporate securities and OATs (now merged with Euroclear).

Simple interest   Interest calculated on the assumption that there is no opportunity to reinvest the interest payments during the life of an investment and thereby earn extra income.

SIS   SEGA Inter Settle – CSD for Switzerland.

Soft commodities   Description given to commodities such as sugar, coffee and cocoa, traded through LIFFE since its incorporation of the former London Commodity Exchange (LCE).

Sovereign debt securities   Bonds issued by the government of a country.

SPAN   Standardized Portfolio Analysis of Risk. A form of margin calculation which is used by various clearing organizations.

Speculation   A deal undertaken because the dealer expects prices to move in his favour and thereby realize a profit.

Speculator   The speculator is a trader who wants to assume risk for potentially much higher rewards.

Sponsored member   Type of CREST member whose name appears on the register but has no computer link with CREST.

Spot delivery   A delivery or settlement of currencies on the value date, two business days later.

Spot market   Market for immediate as opposed to future delivery. In the spot market for foreign exchange, settlement is in two business days ahead.

Spot month   The first month for which futures contracts are available.

Spot rate The price prevailing in the spot market.

Spread (1) The difference between bid and asked price on a security. (2) Difference between yield on or prices of two securities of different types or maturities. (3) In underwriting, difference between price realized by an issuer and price paid by the investor. (4) Difference between two prices or two rates. What commodities traders would refer to as the basis.

Stamp duty Tax on purchase of equities in the UK.

Stamp Duty Reserve Tax (SDRT) (UK) Tax payable on the purchase of UK equities in uncertified form (i.e. those held within CREST).

Standard settlement instructions Instructions for settlement with a particular counterparty which are always followed for a particular kind of deal and, once in place, are therefore not repeated at the time of each transaction.

Standing instruction Default instruction, e.g. provided to an agent processing payments or clearing securities trades; provided by shareholder on how to vote shares (for example, vote for all management recommended candidates).

Stanza di compensazione Italian clearing organization.

Stock In some countries (e.g. the USA), the term applies to ordinary share capital of a company. In other countries (e.g. the UK), stock may mean share capital that is issued in variable amounts instead of in fixed specified amounts, or it can describe government loans.

Stock dividend Dividends paid by a company in stock instead of cash.

Stock Exchange Automated Quotation System (SEAQ) Electronic screen display system through which market-makers in equities display prices at which they are willing to deal.

Stock Index Futures/Options Based on the value of an underlying stock index such as the FTSE 100 in the UK, the S&P 500 index in the USA and the Nikkei 225 and 300 in Japan. Delivery is fulfilled by the payment or receipt of cash against the exchange calculated delivery settlement price. These are referred to as both indices or indexes.

Stock (order)   An owner of a physical security that has been mutilated, lost or stolen will request the issuer to place a stop (transfer) on the security and to cancel and replace the security.

Stock (or bond) power   A legal document, either on the back of registered stocks and bonds or attached to them, by which the owner assigns his interest in the corporation to a third party, allowing that party the right to substitute another name on the company records instead of the original owner's.

Stock split   When a corporation splits its stock, it divides.

Straight debt   A standard bond issue, without right to convert into the common shares of the issuer.

Straightthrough processing   Computer transmission of the details of a trade, without manual intervention, from their original input by the trader to all other relevant areas – position keeping, risk control, accounts, settlement, reconciliation.

Street name   Securities held in street name are held in the name of a broker or another nominee, i.e. a customer.

Strike price   The fixed price, per share or unit, at which an option conveys the right to call (purchase) or put (sell) the underlying shares or units.

Strike price/rate   Also exercise price. The price or rate at which the holder of an option can insist on the underlying transaction being fulfilled.

Stripped bonds (strips)   Bonds where the rights to the interest payments and eventual repayment of the nominal value have been separated from each other and trade independently. Facility introduced for gilts in December 1997.

Sub-custodian   A bank in a foreign country that acts on behalf of the custodian as its custody agent.

Subscription price   Price at which shareholders of a corporation are entitled to purchase common shares in a rights offering or at which subscription warrants are exercisable.

Subscriptions   In a bond issue, the buying orders from the lead manager, co-managers, underwriters and selling group members for the securities being offered.

Stump period   A calculation period, usually at the beginning or end of a swap, other than the standard ones normally quoted.

Swap   Arrangement where two borrowers, one of whom has fixed interest and one of whom has floating rate borrowings, swap their commitments with each other. A bank would arrange the swap and charge a fee.

SwapClear   A clearing house and central counterparty for swaps.

SwapsWire   An electronic dealing system for swaps.

SWIFT   Society for Worldwide Interbank Financial Telecommunications – secure electronic communications network between banks.

TARGET   Trans European Automated Real time Gross settlement Express Transfer – system linking the real-time gross settlements for euros in the 15 European Union countries.

Tax reclaim   The process that a global custodian and/or a holder of securities performs, in accordance with local government filing requirements, in order to recapture an allowable percentage of tax withheld.

Termination date   The end date of a swap.

Thomson Report   An electronic transaction reporting system for international equities on the London Stock Exchange operated by Thomson.

Tick size   The value of a one-point movement in the contract price.

Time value   The amount by which an option's premium exceeds its intrinsic value. Where an option has no intrinsic value the premium consists entirely of time value.

Trade date   The date on which a trade is made.

Trade guarantees   Guarantees in place in a market which ensure that all compared or netted trades will be settled as compared regardless of a counterparty default.

Traded option   An option which is traded on an exchange.

Trader   An individual who buys and sells securities with the objective of making short-term gains.

Transfer agent   Agent appointed by a corporation to maintain records of stock and bond owners, to cancel and issue certificates and to resolve problems arising from lost, destroyed or stolen certificates.

Transfer form   Document which owners of registered documents must sign when they sell the security. Not required where a book entry transfer system is in use.

Transparency   The degree to which a market is characterized by prompt availability of accurate price and volume information which gives participants comfort that the market is fair.

TRAX   Trade confirmation system for the Euromarkets operated by ISMA.

Treasury bill   Money market instrument issued with a life of less than one year issued by the US and UK governments.

Treasury bonds (USA)   US government bond issued with a 30-year maturity.

Treasury notes (USA)   US government bond issued with 2-, 3-, 5- and 7-year maturity.

Triple A rating   The highest credit rating for a bond or company – the risk of default (or non-payment) is negligible.

Trustee   A person appointed to oversee the management of certain funds. They are responsible for ensuring that the fund is managed correctly and that the interests of the investor are protected and that all relevant regulations and legislation are complied with.

Turnaround   Securities bought and sold for settlement on the same day.

Turnaround time   The time available or needed to settle a turnaround trade.

Underlying asset   The asset from which the future or option's price is derived.

Undersubscribed   Circumstance when people have applied for fewer shares than are available in a new issue.

Unrealized profit   Profit which has not arisen from a sale – an increase in value of an asset.

Value at Risk (VaR)   The maximum amount which a bank expects to lose, with a given confidence level, over a given time period.

Variation margin   The process of revaluing an exchange-traded product each day. It is the difference between the closing price on the previous day against the current closing price. It is physically paid or received each day by the clearing organization. It is often referred to as the mark-to-market.

Volatility   The degree of scatter of the underlying price when compared to the mean average rate.

Warrant   An option which can be listed on an exchange, with a lifetime of generally more than one year.

Warrant agent   A bank appointed by the issuer as an intermediary between the issuing company and the (physical) warrant holders, interacting when the latter want to exercise the warrants.

Withholding tax   In the securities industry, a tax imposed by a government's tax authorities on dividends and interest paid.

Writer   A person who has sold an open derivatives contract and is obliged to deliver or take delivery upon notification of exercise from the buyer.

XETRA   Dealing system of the Deutsche Börse.

Yield   Internal rate of return expressed as a percentage.

Yield curve   For securities that expose the investor to the same credit risk, a graph showing the relationship at a given point in the time between yield and current maturity. Yield curves are typically drawn using yields on governments of various maturities.

Yield to maturity   The rate of return yielded by a debt security held to maturity when both interest payments and the investor's capital gain or loss on the security are taken into account.

Zero coupon bond   A bond issued with no coupon but a price substantially below par so that only capital is accrued over the life of the loan, and yield is comparable to coupon-bearing instruments.

Index

Page numbers in italic refer to figures

SECURITIES INSTITUTE

Qualifications

Securities Institute Diploma – the professional qualification for practitioners leading to Fellowship of the Institute

Investment Advice Certificate – the benchmark examination for financial advisors

SFA Registered Persons Examination – the benchmark examinations for employees of SFA regulated firms

Investment Administration Qualification – the benchmark examination for administration, operations and IT staff

International Capital Markets Qualification – the introductory qualification for overseas and emerging markets

Membership

Professionalism through a progressive structure of recognised designations: SIAff, MSI, FSI

Over 17,000 students, affiliates, members and fellows

Free membership events, providing education and networking opportunities

Examination qualification programmes

Continuing Learning opportunities through a wide range of courses and conferences with discounts available for members

Training, Continuing Learning & Publications for the financial services industry

The courses, seminars and publications we produce are researched and developed by working closely with market practitioners and employers to produce focussed, high quality and value-for-money training solutions that meet the needs of busy professionals.

To find out more about all our products and services, please call the Marketing Department on *020 7645 0670*, email us on *marketing@securities-institute.org.uk*, or visit our web site:

www.securities–institute.org.uk

Centurion House, 24 Monument Street, London, EC3R 8AQ

PROFESSIONALISM | INTEGRITY | EXCELLENCE